PowerShell

A Beginner's Guide to Windows PowerShell

Roger Wilson

Table of Contents

Introduction 1

Chapter One: What is Windows PowerShell 3

Chapter Two: How to Use PowerShell 7

Chapter Three: Commands in PowerShell 18

Chapter Four: Objects in PowerShell 31

Chapter Five: The Pipeline 41

Chapter Six: Scripting in PowerShell 73

Chapter Seven: Advanced Cmdlets in PowerShell 85

Final Words 90

Introduction

Windows PowerShell is a scripting language and automation engine that is designed using object-oriented concepts with the .NET framework. It provides a Graphical User Interface (GUI) and command line components to manipulate servers and workstations using a scripting language that offers easy syntax. PowerShell works simply by invoking cmdlets and scripts locally or remotely. PowerShell uses the background Intelligent Transfer Service (BITS) to transfer files between machines in an asynchronized and prioritized manner.

PowerShell has several advantages, including the ability to execute powerful scripts to accomplish tasks that cannot be executed using a few lines of code. Further, PowerShell variables can hold output from values, commands, and objects, and it is not necessary to specify the type of a particular variable.

PowerShell holds advantages over the traditional command line interface in several respects. First, it is integrated with the Windows operating system and provides a scripting language and interactive command line interface to execute scripts. On the other hand, the command line interface is a simple Win32 application provided by Microsoft, and it can interact with any Win32 application. Cmdlets used in PowerShell are not available through the command prompt and can be invoked by the automation scripts or the runtime environment. Cmdlets in PowerShell are treated as objects, and this provides the flexibility to use them anywhere else by passing them as input to another cmdlet. This feature is only specific to PowerShell, which also consists of several other capabilities, features, and functions that are not available in the command prompt with only very basic functionality.

PowerShell is increasingly becoming the preferred scripting platform for IT administrators as it supports management operations in large corporate networks containing as many as four hundred servers. Functions, like executing security solutions that require a script to be constantly running in the background, can be accomplished with PowerShell scripting. It allows comprehensive functionality, including the ability to login to multiple servers to check whether a specific service is installed and running. These otherwise time-consuming operations can be completed in much less time and limit human error as the time spent doing non-productive processes is minimized. Tasks can be completed in only a few minutes as scripts may be used to complete operations related to services executing on multiple servers.

These are just a few examples of the benefits and features of PowerShell. Throughout the following chapters we will take a deep dive into PowerShell scripting and discuss in more detail how to use PowerShell effectively. Let's begin!

Chapter One: What is Windows PowerShell

PowerShell is a task automation solution that works across platforms. It helps automate tasks in the Windows ecosystem and simplifies configuration, like exchange and active directory. It has the capability to handle large file batches, assist in setting up new machines, control access to large file volume, and automate the tasks related to adding network drives, taking backups, updating security software, and granting users access to shared files.

The most frequent automation tasks performed using PowerShell are working with file batches to control access to a large number of files and automate backups, adding and removing new users, updating security software, adding network drives, granting access to shared files, displaying the USB devices on computers on a network, setting an elaborate task to run as a background process, terminating non-responsive processes, and filtering information about computers in a network for exporting it in HTML format.

PowerShell consists of a scripting language, configuration management framework, and command-line shell. Compatible with macOS, Windows, and Linux, it is a high-level programming language developed by Microsoft to automate configurations and actions.

The Command Shell

The command shell in PowerShell is unlike any other platform. While most shells accept and return text, PowerShell returns .NET objects. The shell consists of a number of features: command and parameter aliases, pipeline for chaining commands, in-console help system, command prediction, tab completion, and a robust command-line history.

The Scripting Language

PowerShell can be used as a scripting language to automate the management of systems and to deploy solutions in continuous integration/continuous delivery (CI/CD) environments. PowerShell scripting language is fully extensible with its classes, modules, scripts, and functions. Its formatting system is also extensible and gives easy access to output. An extensible type system helps to create dynamic types. Further, it supports built-in data formats, like JSON, CSV, and XML. PowerShell is built on .NET common language runtime and takes .NET objects as inputs and outputs. It does not require parsing of text output to extract information from the output.

Configuration Management Environment

The configuration management environment used by PowerShell is the PowerShell Desired State Configuration (DSC) and enables the management of enterprise infrastructure using configuration as the code. DSC helps you to create declarative configurations and custom scripts that may be used for deployments again and again. It is possible to deploy configuration with PowerShell's push and pull models. Furthermore, it allows the enforcement of configuration settings and reporting on configuration drift.

The PowerShell Studio 2021

PowerShell Studio 2021 is the integrated environment for making tools and scripting. It has an editor with many features and supports code formatting and script debugging. It offers several functions, such as the ability to create windows services, modules, functions, and installers. In addition, it has several other features, including monitoring the performance of scripts and memory usage, debugging multiple files and modules at the same time, and the file recovery feature.

The PowerShell Studio makes life easy for developers as graphical tools can be easily created using the GUI designer, saving the time and effort required to write hundreds of lines of code. PowerShell allows you to create controls and templates easily with advanced GUI features. It not only allows you to create modules but also allows you to convert existing functions to distributable modules. All these functions can be accomplished easily with powerful features, such as reference highlighting, syntax coloring, code formatting, bookmarking, and code completion.

It also allows you to deliver solutions for your chosen environment by using the script packager, which is versatile because it allows you to customize packages according to machine, platform, domain, MAC address, and user. This allows the script to be accessed and executed only by the authorized user. The script packager is comprehensive as it allows you to create MSI installers to distribute executables, scripts, and modules. PowerShell Studio also has built-in performance for your script, so you know exactly how your script is performing in terms of CPU usage and real-time use of memory.

Chapter Summary

- PowerShell works across platforms and is mainly targeted at task automation.

- It has a broad range of capabilities, including handling large file volume, automating network tasks, manipulating shared files, and keeping security software up to date.

- The three main components of PowerShell are a scripting language, a command shell, and a configuration management environment.

- While the command shell is useful for executing commands and the scripting language helps design simple and complex scripts, the configuration management environment is useful in managing enterprise infrastructure.

- The PowerShell studio 2021 is an integrated environment that also features an editor to format code and debug scripts. It has several features, such as the ability to create windows services and modules, monitor memory usage and script performance, and many more functions.

Chapter Two: How to Use PowerShell

The PowerShell language is a high-level proprietary programming language developed by Microsoft that enables system administrators to automate configurations and actions. Administrators commonly utilize PowerShell to work with Active Directory. The language can be used in the Windows environment and is based on object-oriented concepts. It is possible to automate repetitive and tedious tasks through PowerShell scripts containing multiple commands. PowerShell for Windows is analogous to Bash Scripting in Linux.

The main component of PowerShell is the cmdlet that may be used to manage computers from the command line. Users are able to access data stores, such as the Certificate Store and the Registry, similar to accessing the file system. PowerShell ISE, its Integrated Scripting Environment, is layered on top of PowerShell, which allows creation and running of commands and modification of test scripts without the need to type commands to accomplish the purpose.

PowerShell can be invoked by clicking on the Windows icon on the lower left-hand corner of the screen then typing "PowerShell". This displays the PowerShell command prompt as shown below:

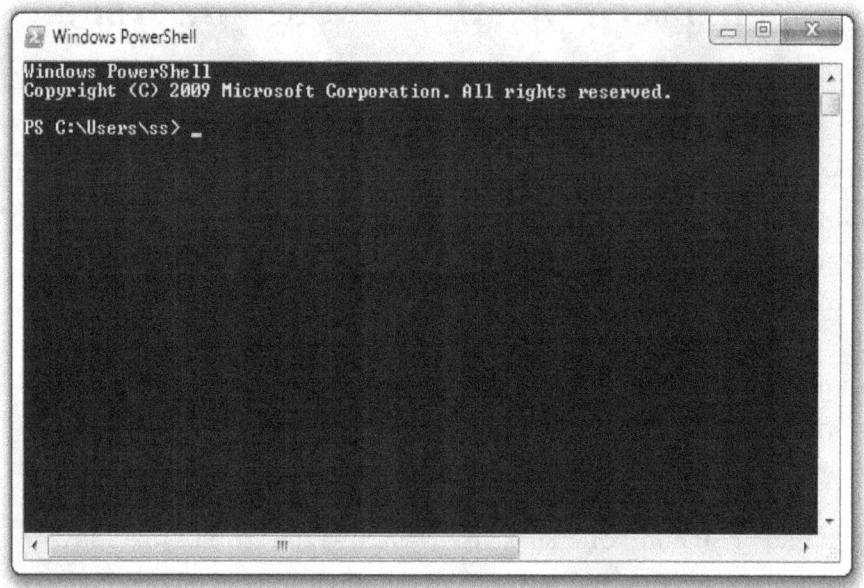

PowerShell was developed for configuration management and task automation and was later converted into an open-source platform. It is available for multiple platforms, including Linux, Windows, and MacOS. It has the .NET framework backbone, and its functions are written in C#. A function in PowerShell is referred to as "cmdlet" and contains functions that return a .NET object. Some basic cmdlets are pre-configured with PowerShell, such as those designed to move or copy files and traverse folders.

As mentioned earlier, PowerShell has the Integrated Scripting Environment (ISE) that makes scripting robust and easy. The PowerShell ISE resembles a command prompt window and contains code-writing functionality. System administrators can use cmdlets and modules to write code. It contains a debugging tool that allows you to test code and identify bugs to fix them. Users can customize PowerShell ISE by selecting a specific font, theme, and color scheme to write scripts. PowerShell has simple commands and syntax.

PowerShell ISE can be invoked by clicking the Windows icon on the lower left corner of the screen and typing "PowerShell ISE".

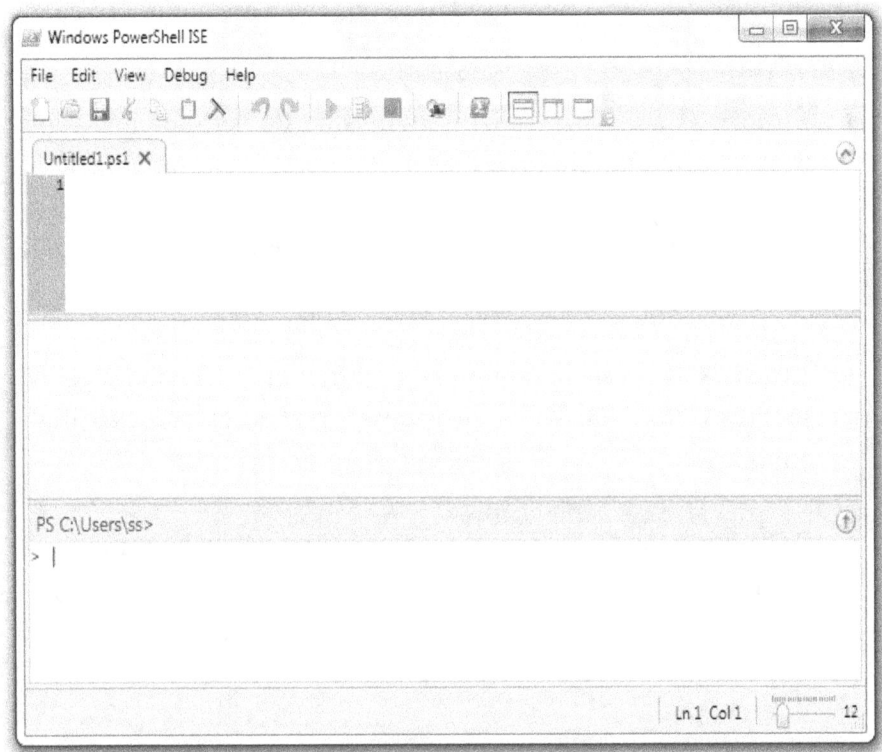

PowerShell has been developed over the years, and since 2006, several versions have been made available. It was first released for Windows XP, Windows Vista, and Windows Server 2003. In 2016, PowerShell 5.1 was made available for Windows Server 2016, and was also included in the Windows 10 Anniversary update. PowerShell is also compatible with Windows Server 2012, Windows Server 2012 R2, Windows 7 Service Pack 1, Windows Server 2008 R2, and Windows 8.1 Enterprise and Pro editions.

Basic Concepts in PowerShell

PowerShell has several important concepts, including functions, scripts, applications, and cmdlets. These concepts are summarized below:

- **Functions** are commands written using PowerShell and can be written using an Integrated Development Environment (IDE).

- **Scripts** have a .ps1 extension and are stored as text files on the disk.

- **Cmdlets** are built-in commands written in .NET language, such as C# or VB. They allow developers to extend existing cmdlets.

- **Debug** is used to instruct a cmdlet to provide debugging information.

- **Verbose** provides information in greater detail.

- **Scripts** are stored on the disk using the .ps1 extension.

- **Applications** are existing programs written in Windows.

- **Confirm** is used to instruct the cmdlet to give a prompt prior to executing the command.

- **What If** is used to indicate that the cmdlet need not be executed but gives information on what would happen if it were executed.

- **ErrorVariable** specifies a variable that holds information about the error.

- **ErrorAction** tells the cmdlet to perform a specific action in the event of an error. It can be used to tell the cmdlet to either stop, continue, or silently continue and inquire about a specific action.

- **OutBuffer** tells the cmdlet to hold a specific count of objects before the cmdlet is invoked.

- **OutVariable** tells the cmdlet to make use of a specific variable that contains output information.

Features of PowerShell

The features of PowerShell are aliases, cmdlets, pipes, and help commands. These basic commands help you write scripts. However, a considerable complexity is associated with PowerShell, for it is not possible to memorize all components of PowerShell. Tools that help you deal with its complexities include Get-Command, Tab Completion, Command String, and Object Properties.

Tab Completion

Tab completion is a feature that allows you to cycle through the commands by hitting the **TAB** key in the command prompt. This means that there is no need to memorize the spellings of the different commands. The tab completion feature provides recommendations for commands and their paths and flags.

Get-Command

PowerShell has the **Get -Command** feature that allows you to remember a command even when you do not know the name of the command. PowerShell lists all commands with a **VERB-NOUN** syntax. For example, a command may start with a word, such as **Add**, **Set**, **Get**, or **Clear**, and the names of the servers and files are accompanied with the verb. **Get -Command** helps discover the commands on your system.

Command String

PowerShell provides the ability to execute commands using a specific syntax to accomplish common functions, like finding a specific path within a file string. It provides all the capabilities available in the traditional command prompt, such as using loop, specific flags, patterns, and the ability to present the output of a particular script. However, PowerShell has simple syntax to complete the same operation. For example, to get all subdirectories under a directory, the path may be provided with the **Get** command, and a filter may also be provided to execute the necessary steps:

Get -ChildItem -Path D:\MyFolder -Filter 'MyFile*'

The example above provides all files available at the target location indicated, which start with 'MyFile'. The wildcard character indicates that the file name should start with 'MyFile'.

```
PS C:\Users\ss> Get-ChildItem -Path D:\MyFolder -Filter 'MyFile*'

    Directory: D:\MyFolder

Mode                LastWriteTime     Length Name
----                -------------     ------ ----
-a---         6/30/2021  12:20 AM          0 MyFile.txt
-a---         6/30/2021  12:20 AM          0 MyFile1.txt
-a---         6/30/2021  12:20 AM          0 MyFile2.txt

PS C:\Users\ss>
```

Object Properties

PowerShell also has a way to provide structured output instead of big strings that are less readable. For example, the traditional **ping** command is **Test -Connection** in PowerShell and contains designated columns to show the source, destination, IP address, byes, and time taken. It is also possible to pass this information to another command and execute the same or make small modifications.

Basic Punctuation in PowerShell

PowerShell uses a few characters to perform frequent functions:

- The $ sign is used for variable declaration.
- "" are used to display output.
- = is used to assign a value to a variable.

- () creates an argument.
- + concatenates two strings.

Cmdlets in PowerShell

Command lets or cmdlets in PowerShell are lightweight commands used in the Windows PowerShell Environment. The command prompt can be used to invoke and execute cmdlets. Cmdlets are not simply commands as in the other programming languages. They are objects of the .NET framework that can be created using a few lines of code and can be executed separately. Cmdlets process a single object at a time and process objects. However, it is not possible to use them to format output, for parsing, or presentation of errors. PowerShell cmdlets are in the noun-verb format, separated by a hyphen. **Get** (get something), **Set** (define something), **Out** (give an output), **Stop** (stop something that is running), **Start** (run something), and **New** (create something) are some common keywords in PowerShell that occur frequently in cmdlets. Some examples of commands include: **Get -Help,** which provides help on the PowerShell topics and commands; **Get -Service [word]**, which is used to find all commands containing the specified [word]; **Get -Command**, which gets information about the thing that is invoked; and **Get -Member**, which displays what can be done with an object.

Data Types in PowerShell

PowerShell consists of a number of data types, such as Integer, Boolean, Date, Byte, and many more as indicated below:

- **Byte** defines an 8-bit unsigned whole number from 0 to 255.
- **Decimal** is a 128-bit decimal value.

- **Long** defines a 64-bit signed whole number, which is similar to an integer but can hold a larger value.

- **Short** is a 16-bit unsigned integer, which is similar to an integer but can take fewer values. It can take values between -32,768 and +32,768.

- **Boolean** specifies a true or false condition.

- **Char** is a 16-bit unsigned number that can take values between 0 and 63,535.

- **Date** represents a date in the calendar.

- **Double** is a 64-bit double precision floating point number but with a narrower range of values when compared to the decimal.

- **Integer** is a 32-bit whole number.

- **String** represents a text, which is a group of characters.

- **Single** represents a single-precision floating point number containing 32 bits. Single is similar to the **Double** data type but holds fewer values.

- **Short** is an unsigned integer containing 16-bits. Although it is similar to the **Integer** data type, it holds far fewer values.

Special Variables in PowerShell

PowerShell consists of several special variables such as the ones described below:

- **$PID** stores the process identifier.
- **$False** contains the FALSE value.
- **$True** contains the TRUE value.
- **$Error** represents an array of error objects.
- **$Profile** stores the path of the user profile in the default shell.
- **$Host** displays the name of the host application in use currently.
- **$NULL** contains an empty value or NULL value.
- **$PSUICulture** contains the current UI culture name.

Chapter Summary

- PowerShell is based on object-oriented concepts.

- It is analogous to Bash scripting in the Linux operating system.

- Most of the operations in PowerShell are carried out using cmdlets.

- PowerShell can be simply invoked by clicking the Windows icon on the lower left corner of the screen and typing "PowerShell".

- Complex or elaborate code can be written in PowerShell using its Integrated Scripting Environment (ISE).

- The main components of PowerShell are its functions, cmdlets, scripts, and applications.

- PowerShell also includes powerful functions, such as Get-Command, Tab-Completion, Object Properties, and Command String.
- Cmdlets are light-weight commands in PowerShell.

- PowerShell works with a range of datatypes from Decimal, Byte, Date, Char, and Integer, to Short, Single, Double, and many more.

- PowerShell also works with several special variables, such as $Host, $NULL, $Error, and many more.

Chapter Three: Commands in PowerShell

PowerShell is developed using the IEEE POSIX standard for the Korn Shell, which also forms the foundation for Zsh and Bash. It is designed using C# and can be used to write complex scripts. Commands form the fundamental units of PowerShell, and its syntax is similar to the one indicated below

command -parameter1 -parameter2 argument1 argument2

Command is the name of the command. The command name is followed by **parameters**, which may be switch parameters, regular parameters, or positional parameters. Parameters may or may not have **arguments**. Switch parameters do not take any arguments. Regular parameters take arguments. Positional parameters are those whose matching parameter is inferred by the position of the argument. In the example above, **command** is the name of the command, **-parameter1** is the switch parameter, **-parameter2 arg1** is the parameter with the argument, and **arg2** is the positional argument.

PowerShell has different commands, including shell function commands, cmdlets, workflow commands, script commands, and native Windows commands. The command name is followed by zero or more parameters and arguments. The dash (-) precedes a parameter, which is accompanied by the name of the parameter. On the other hand, an argument is the value associated with a specific parameter. An example of a command is:

Write-Output -InputObject Hello

In this example, **Write-Output** is the command, **-InputObject** is the parameter, and **Hello** is the argument. Another example of the same command is indicated below:

Write-Output Hello

Here, the output is **Hello** as it is specified as **-InputObject**. PowerShell has an intelligent interpreter, known as the **parameter binder**, which does not require all information for that parameter. The parameter binder also matches argument type to parameter type. The output for these commands is displayed below.

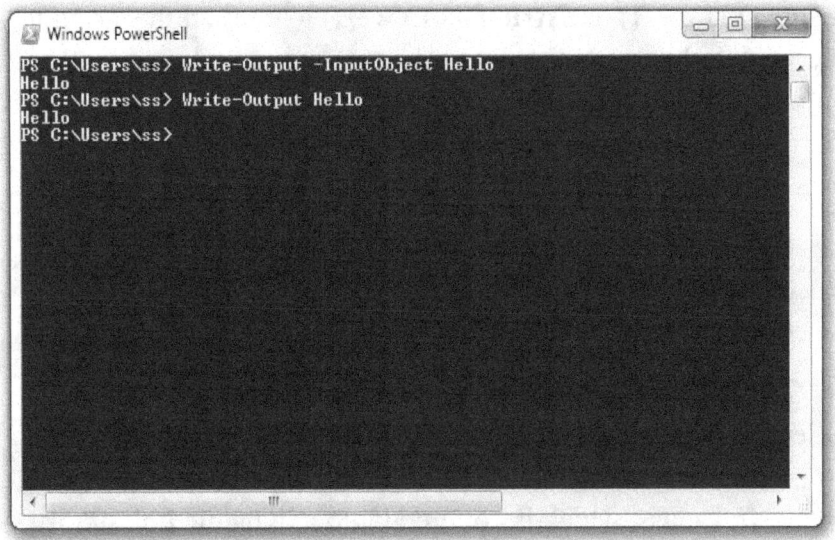

PowerShell uses a type-conversion system that is quite complex. The type-convertor converts the strings to the correct type of parameter or gives an error message that says the type conversion has failed. For example, the following commands give the same output:

Write-Output -InputObject "-InputObject"

Write-Output "-InputObject"

PowerShell also allows you to specify an **end of parameters** parameter, which is a double hyphen (--). When the PowerShell interpreter encounters this **end of parameters** parameter, it treats the rest of the sequence as an argument even though it may look like a parameter.

PowerShell also provides the option to assign this output to a string preceded by a $ sign, such as **$str = Write-Output `Hello, World`**. The output of commands can be further scrutinized by sending it to the **Get-member** cmdlet in a pipeline. It is also possible to call different methods on an object using the "dot notation," such as **$string.ToUpper()** or **$string.ToLower()** to convert the string to upper case or lowercase respectively. Another popular method is the **Replace()** method, which when applied to a string can replace the occurrence of a specific word with another one. It also allows you to create your custom objects, such as the HashTable.

Types of Commands in PowerShell

The four types of commands in PowerShell are functions, cmdlets, Win32 executables, and scripts. Some versions of PowerShell, like v4, also have configurations. Cmdlets are derived from a .NET class, which is compiled into a dynamic link library (DLL) and loaded into the PowerShell process at startup. Cmdlets are the most efficient commands. The verb-noun pair of cmdlets function similarly to the built-in commands and can be added at runtime.

<u>Function</u>: Functions in PowerShell have parameters similar to cmdlets but have some limitations. The parameter specification capabilities of functions and scripts are similar to those offered by cmdlets, as the structure of their commands is the same. The streaming behavior of functions is also similar to that of cmdlets.

Workflow: PowerShell workflows are another feature that were introduced in PowerShell v3. The syntax of workflows is similar to functions. When a workflow is loaded into memory, a function is created and can be viewed through PowerShell drive.

Script: In PowerShell, a script is a piece of PowerShell code that is saved with a .ps1 extension and loaded into the memory and parsed at the time of its execution. When a script runs, it is slower than a function when it starts, but gets to the same speed during execution. Moreover, script commands and shell function commands are the same.

Native Commands: Native commands are external executable programs that can be handled by the operating system. Native commands require the creation of a new process and run quite slowly. Their syntax is different from other types of commands, and they do their own parameter processing. Native commands can be used to accomplish a wide variety of behaviors. The most obvious example of a native command is the PowerShell interpreter, which is invoked by giving the command **powershell.exe**. Executing **powershell.exe** calls an interpreter from within PowerShell by creating a second process, which is a child process. The ability to run child processes in PowerShell allows scripts to be embedded inline. Fragments of scripts can be embedded into the main script by delimiting it with braces. An example is shown below:

powershell { Get-Process System } | Format-Table Handles, Id, ProcessName -Autosize

The script above contains an embedded child process **Get-Process System**. This code executes and displays the specific properties related to the process, such as **Id**, **ProcessName**, and

Handles. The **-AutoSize** attribute is used to size the columns for a convenient display. The output is formatted as a table with these three columns. The advantage of executing in this way is that the output is available as serialized objects, which can be passed to other commands.

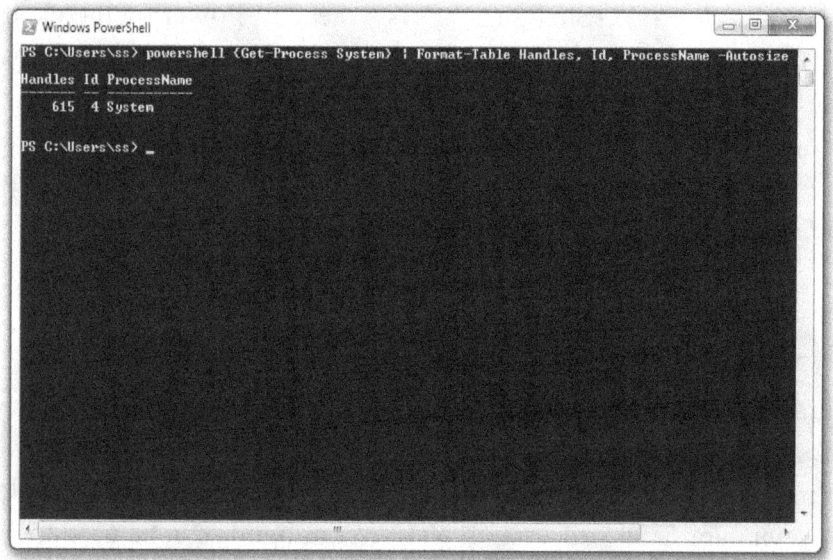

Launching PowerShell

PowerShell can be launched in Windows 10 using the search field. The search text field is available from the taskbar, and PowerShell can be accessed by typing **powershell** and clicking on **Windows PowerShell**. It is also possible to run PowerShell with administrator privileges. To do so, right click on **Windows PowerShell** in the search results and click **Run as Administrator**.

Creating and Running Scripts

PowerShell scripts are saved with the extension ".ps1". It is not possible to run this script by just double-clicking the file. To run PowerShell scripts, right click on the file with the **.ps1** extension and click "Run with PowerShell". However, in order to run scripts, the necessary policies must be set up using **Get -ExecutionPolicy**. This command provides the current status of privileges, which may be one of the following:

AllSigned - It is only possible to run scripts from a trusted developer. Prior to running the script, a prompt is available.

Restricted - Scripts cannot be executed. This is the default setting for Windows. It must be changed.

Unrestricted - You can run any script. This makes the system vulnerable and must not be used.

RemoteSigned - It is possible to run your scripts or those trusted by a developer.

The command used to set the policy to the required level is:

Set-ExecutionPolicy remoteSigned

Running PowerShell Script

PowerShell scripts can be executed in two ways. It is possible to write scripts in notepad using Windows Command Line and the file with the **ps1** extension, then call the script from PowerShell. This enables you to see the output in PowerShell. For example, the following command can be saved with the filename **script.ps1**:

Write-Host "This is the new script"

The script can be executed using PowerShell by giving the command **.\script.ps1** after navigating to the folder where the script is saved. This gives the output in PowerShell.

```
Administrator: Windows PowerShell
PS D:\MyFolder> Set-ExecutionPolicy remoteSigned

Execution Policy Change
The execution policy helps protect you from scripts that you do not trust. Changing the execution policy might expose
you to the security risks described in the about_Execution_Policies help topic. Do you want to change the execution
policy?
[Y] Yes  [N] No  [S] Suspend  [?] Help (default is "Y"): y
PS D:\MyFolder> .\script.ps1
This is the new script
PS D:\MyFolder>
```

Further, it is also possible to execute PowerShell scripts using the Integrated Scripting Environment (ISE), which allows running and executing scripts in a GUI environment. The GUI environment is convenient as it provides several features, such as editing multiple lines at a time, highlighting syntax, selective execution, and tab completion to name a few. It is also possible to work with multiple windows simultaneously. This is a useful feature when one script makes a call to another script.

Basic Commands in PowerShell

PowerShell features cmdlets, which are commands with a predefined function. They work similarly to operators in other programming languages. Cmdlets can be classified as user, system, and custom cmdlets. When a cmdlet is executed, an object or an array of objects is passed in its output. It is possible to analyze data using cmdlets or pass the output, i.e. object(s) of cmdlets to another cmdlet using the pipe operator. Several cmdlets can also be used in a string by separating them using semicolons (;). Finally, cmdlets are not case-sensitive, which means that it does not matter whether you use uppercase or lowercase letters to define and execute the cmdlets.

Some the basic cmdlets used frequently in PowerShell include:

- **Get** - Get something.
- **Start** - Start running something.
- **Set** - Define something.
- **Stop** - Stop a thing that is running.
- **New** - Create something new.
- **Out** - Output something.

The **Get** cmdlet is one of the most common cmdlets used in PowerShell. It can be used to get different types of content, processes, and services with a number of parameters defined in PowerShell. Here are a few basic commands in PowerShell you want to understand to be able to use the **Get** cmdlet effectively:

Get-Process: This cmdlet displays the processes that are currently running on your computer.

Get-Content: The **Get-Content** cmdlet displays the content of the file that you specify as a Windows file path.

Get-Service: The **Get-Service** cmdlet shows the list of services that are currently running along with their status or any other parameters that are specified in the cmdlet syntax.

Get-Command: The **Get-Command** provides a list of all available commands so you can select a suitable command for your precise requirements. The **Get-Command -Type Cmdlet** provides a list of cmdlets available in PowerShell.

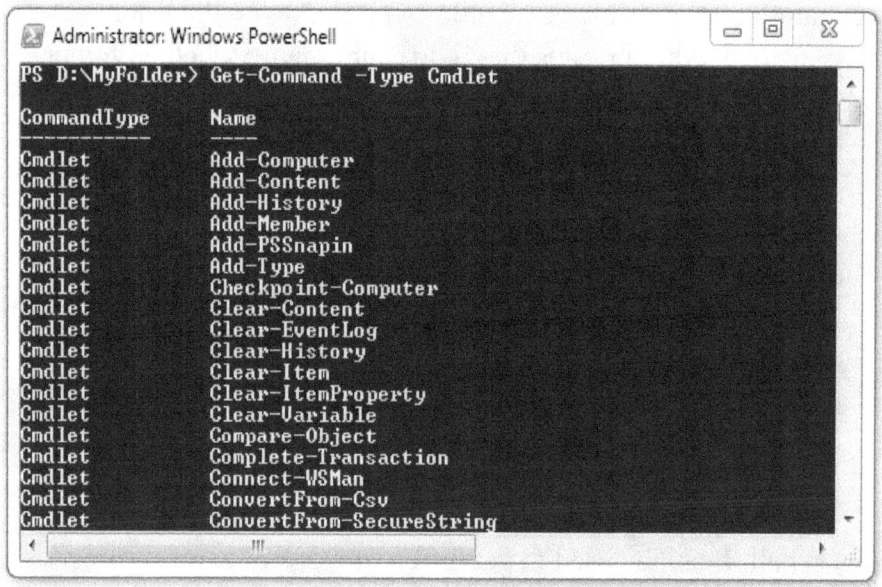

Get-Help: The **Get-Help** command provides more information on using a specific command. Some examples include **Get-Help -Detailed** and **Get-Help -Online**. In this example, **-Detailed** and **-Online** are switches that list information to complete a specific task. Other switches of the **Get-Help** command include **-Full** and **-Examples**.

Get-Module: The **Get-Module** or **Import-Module** gives you access to modules to automate products. **Get-Module -ListAvailable** provides a list of all modules and commands available in it. When considering modules from vendors, download and install the module prior to running the **Get -Module** cmdlet. Modules that have been installed can be imported using **Import -Module**. To view cmdlets included in the module use the **Get-Command -Module**.

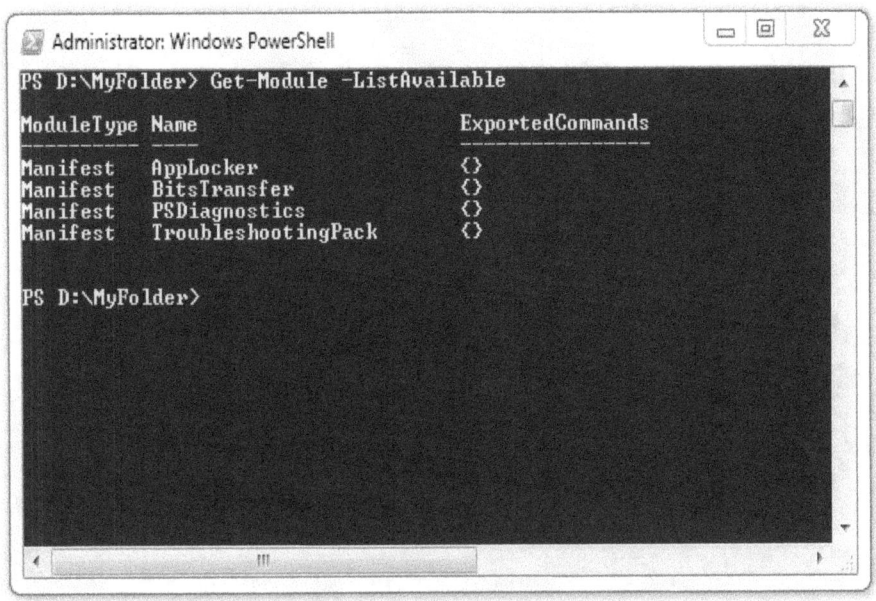

Get-Member: The **Get-Member** command shows all properties, methods, and member types. On the other hand, the **Format-List** command provides information that is useful to system administrators and individuals with a high level of technical knowledge.

Command Pipelines

When commands are separated by the | operator, they form a pipeline in PowerShell. Pipelines are a series of commands. The output of one command is passed along to the next command as input. The following command pipeline shows all three types of parameters and the process of passing the output of one command to the other through the use of the | operator:

dir -recurse -filter *.txt | format-table name, length

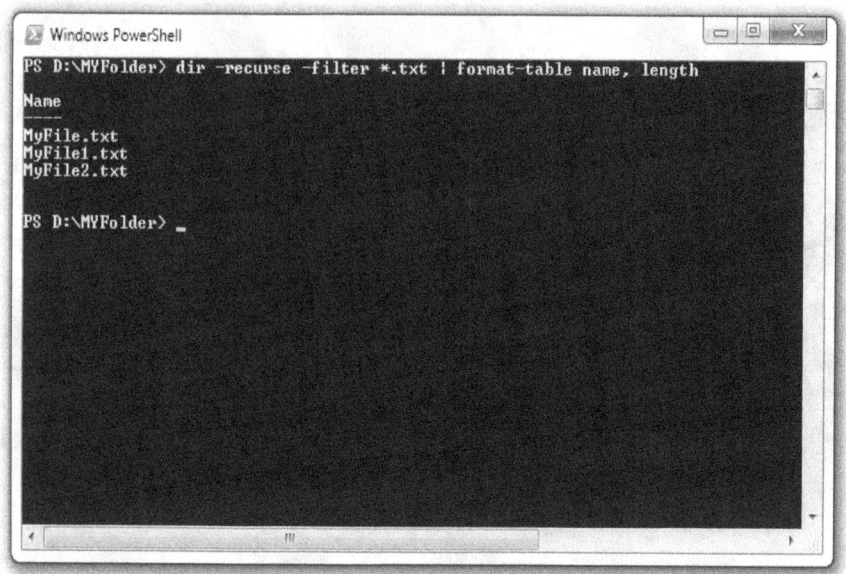

The command used here is **dir** with a switch parameter -**recurse**. **-filter *.txt** is a parameter with an argument. This forms the first command, which gives an output that is passed to another command, **format-table**. The purpose of the second command is to present the output from the first command as a table containing the **name** and **length**. Here, **name, length** is the positional argument. When a command pipeline is supplied to the PowerShell parser, it processes each of the individual commands and provides the result to the next command. Finally, it returns a result after processing all the commands, one after another.

The Parsing Process in PowerShell

Commands in PowerShell can only be executed after they are parsed by the PowerShell interpreter. For example, when a simple expression, such as "3+2", is supplied to the **parser**, it is converted into an internal representation, which is then supplied to the **engine**. This execution engine is the point where the expression is evaluated. In the background, a **tokenizer** breaks up the components of the script into internal representations called tokens, which are processed into specific structures through syntactic analysis. A concept associated with tokenizing is **quoting**, which converts a token (with a special meaning) to a simple string. The following example demonstrates the concept of quoting:

Write-Output '-InputObject'

This script prints the output **-InputObject**. Note that **-InputObject** is a built-in object in PowerShell, but in this case, it is parsed as a string, and the output is displayed as the string itself.

Quoting serves different purposes in PowerShell. For example, it can be used to specify the full path of the file present at a specific location. The script **Set-Location 'c:\program files'** refers to the location specified there. When the script **Get-Location** is executed, the path set in the previous instance is executed. However, when you try to accomplish the same task without using quotes, **c:\program** and **files** are treated as different tokens, and an error is produced.

Chapter Summary

- The standard used to develop PowerShell was the IEEE POSIX of the Korn Shell. The IEEE POSIX standard was also the base standard for the design of Bash and Zsh shells.

- PowerShell has several cmdlets, including **Write-Output**, **Get-Process**, and **Format-Table**.

- The main types of commands in PowerShell are scripts, workflows, functions, and native commands.

- To be able to execute scripts in PowerShell, it is important to set up the required permissions using the **Get-ExecutionPolicy** cmdlet and specifying **remoteSigned** as the privilege (**Set-ExecutionPolicy remoteSigned**).

- The most frequently used cmdlets in PowerShell are **Stop**, **Set**, **Get**, **Start**, **Out**, and **New**.

- The **Get** cmdlet can be used to access processes (**Get-Process**), commands (**Get-Command**), services (**Get-Service**), and many more.

- PowerShell uses command pipelines to feed the objects from one cmdlet to the next one and achieve the desired output.

- Commands in PowerShell are executed after they are parsed by the PowerShell interpreter.

Chapter Four: Objects in PowerShell

PowerShell has **types** and **classes**. An example is the robin, a bird, which can be considered a **type** belonging to the **parent class** of bird. Birds have many **properties** such as feathers, beak, and the ability to fly. This example gives insight into how object-oriented programming works. Here, a **type** is the description of an **object**, and the two have a **relationship**. In this example, a relationship may be defined as "Robin is a bird". A **class** in PowerShell is used to define a new **type**. Classes have **behaviors** that are defined using **methods**. When referring to all properties and methods, the term **member** may be used. When an action is performed on an **object**, it is possible to trigger a special method called an **event**. For example, a method that instructs the bird to fly may internally trigger another event to swoop on prey while flying.

Objects also have **schemas**, which are the template for that object. This is also known as the **type** of the object and may be perceived as its **blueprint**. The type of the object is defined by a **class**. When we say that Robin is a bird, we mean that Robin is the **class**, and bird is the **type**.

Getting Object Members

The information associated with **objects** is referred to as **members**. Cmdlets allow you to get this information. The **Get-Member** cmdlet allows you to find properties and methods for a specific object. In the following example, the members returned by the **Get-Service** cmdlet is passed to the **Get-Member** using a command pipeline as shown below:

Get-Service -ServiceName 'BITS' | Get-Member

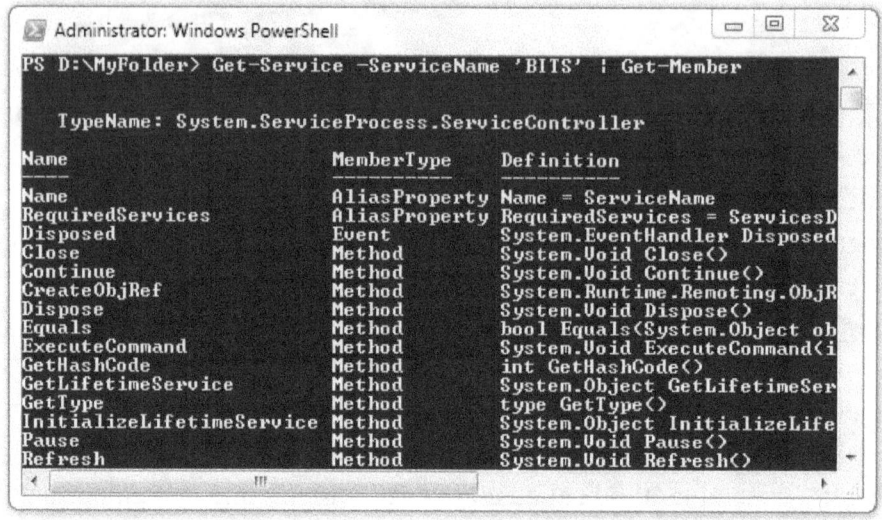

Properties or attributes of an object can be retrieved by using the following command. The **Get-Member** cmdlet is used to find the property names as shown below:

Get-Service | Get-Member -MemberType Property

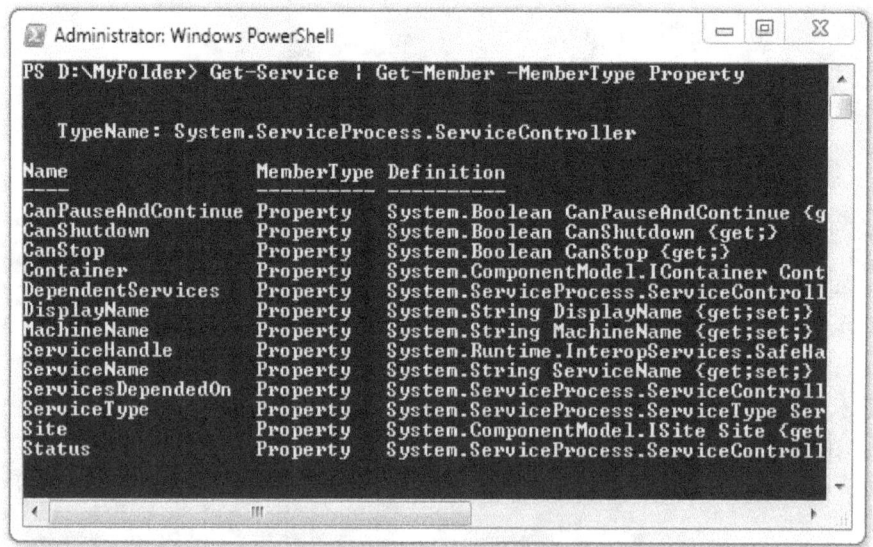

To find property values, the following command may be executed:

Get-Service -ServiceName 'BITS' | Select-Object -Property 'StartType'

Aliases are intuitive names for properties. Aliases may be used to refer to the value of a property instead of using the actual name of the property. Take the following example:

Get-Service | Get-Member -MemberType 'AliasProperty'

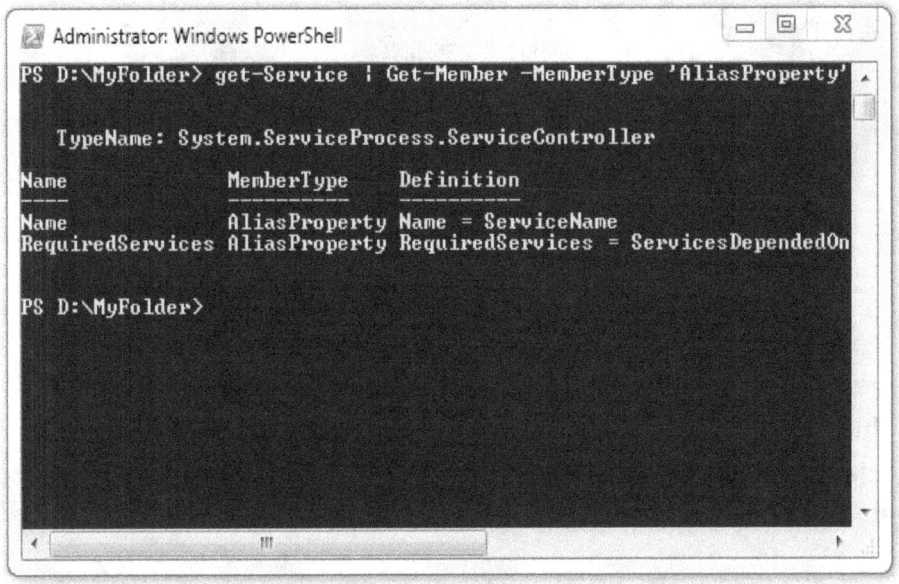

The methods of an object are the actions that can be performed on it. The **Get-member** cmdlet lets you view the methods associated with an object. The following command displays all methods:

Get-Service | Get-Member -MemberType 'Method'

```
Administrator: Windows PowerShell
PS D:\MyFolder> Get-Service | Get-Member -MemberType 'Method'

   TypeName: System.ServiceProcess.ServiceController

Name                      MemberType   Definition
----                      ----------   ----------
Close                     Method       System.Void Close()
Continue                  Method       System.Void Continue()
CreateObjRef              Method       System.Runtime.Remoting.ObjRef
Dispose                   Method       System.Void Dispose()
Equals                    Method       bool Equals(System.Object obj)
ExecuteCommand            Method       System.Void ExecuteCommand(int
GetHashCode               Method       int GetHashCode()
GetLifetimeService        Method       System.Object GetLifetimeServic
GetType                   Method       type GetType()
InitializeLifetimeService Method       System.Object InitializeLifetim
Pause                     Method       System.Void Pause()
Refresh                   Method       System.Void Refresh()
Start                     Method       System.Void Start(), System.Voi
Stop                      Method       System.Void Stop()
ToString                  Method       string ToString()
```

Objects have many types of members besides methods, properties, and aliases, such as Property Sets, Script Property, and Note Property. **Script properties** are used to calculate property values. Further, the **note property** is used in the case of static property names. Finally, **property sets** behave like aliases and contain sets of properties.

There are several ways to work with objects, such as displaying their specific properties, sorting and filtering them, counting and averaging the objects, using loops, and comparing the objects. The following examples illustrate these concepts:

Selecting Specific Properties

Get-Service -ServiceName * | Select-Object -Property 'Status', 'DisplayName'

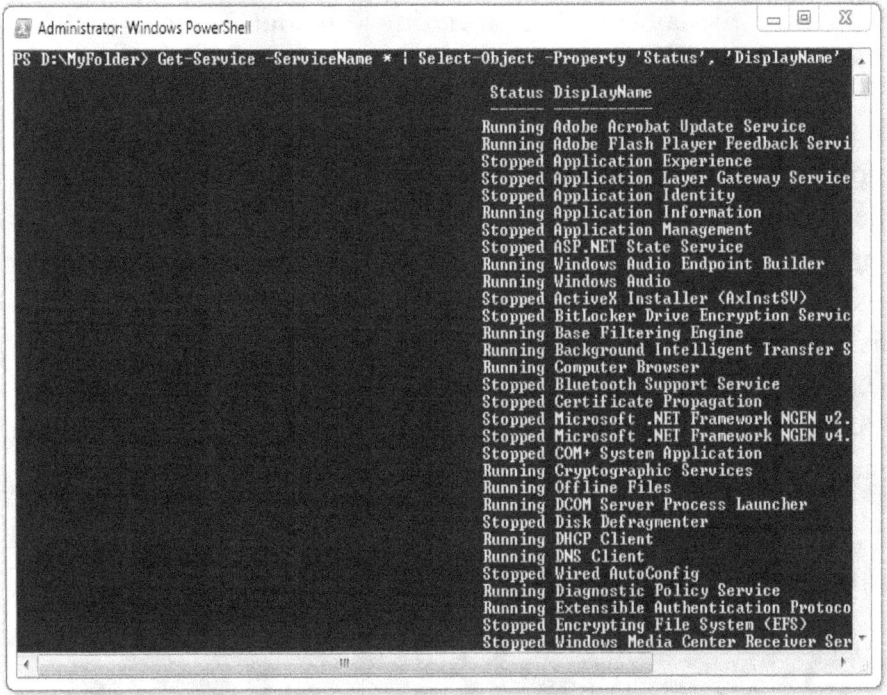

In the command pipeline above, **Get-Service** is the cmdlet that gets all service names. This output is passed to the **Select-Object** cmdlet, which acts as a filter for the available properties and shows the status and display name formatted as a table. This command may be extended to include the sorting and filtering functions as shown below:

Sorting and Formatting the Output

Get-Service * | Select-Object -Property 'Status', 'DisplayName' | Where-Object -FilterScript {$_.Status -eq 'Running' -and $_.DisplayName -like "Windows*"} | Sort-Object -Property 'DisplayName' -Descending | Format-Table -AutoSize

The example above performs several functions using the command pipeline. First, the list of services returned by **Get-Service** cmdlet are passed to the **Select-Object** cmdlet, and the properties are filtered to return only the status and display name. The **Where-Object** cmdlet acts as a filter to filter the services that are running and have "Windows" in their display name. Henceforth, the output from this command pipeline is passed to the **Sort-Object** cmdlet that sorts the result according to the display name (the property) and sorts the output in descending order. Finally, the **Format-Table** cmdlet is used to format the output as a table.

Counting Objects in the Output

It is also possible to count the number of objects returned from a specific command pipeline by using the command pipeline shown below, which contains the **Measure-Object** cmdlet:

Get-Service * | Select-Object -Property 'Status', 'DisplayName' | Where-Object -FilterScript {$_.Status -eq 'Running' -and $_.DisplayName -like "Windows*"} | Sort-Object -Property 'DisplayName' -Descending | Measure-Object

Looping Through the Output

It is also possible to customize the output from a command pipeline using loops as shown in the example below:

Get-Service * | Select-Object -Property 'Status', 'DisplayName' | Where-Object {$_.DisplayName -Like "Windows*" -and $_.Status -eq 'Running'} | Foreach-Object { Write-Host -Foreground-Color 'Yellow' $_.DisplayName "is running" }

The example above uses the **ForEach-Object** cmdlet, which concatenates the string "is running" to every line of the output and changes its color to yellow. The same command can also be used to perform additional actions, like starting and stopping a service. Several other cmdlets can be used to perform different actions on the output, such as **Compare-Object** cmdlet for making a comparison. Given the flexibility and extensibility of command pipelines in PowerShell, you can select any logically valid cmdlets and pass the output of one cmdlet to another to get the desired output.

Chapter Summary

- PowerShell consists of **classes** and **types**. For example, when one refers to robin as a bird, the **type** is robin, and bird is its **parent class**. Alternatively, a type may be referred to as a description of an object.

- The **parent class** bird has **properties** such as feathers, and **relationships**, which is simply stated as "robin is a bird".

- **Classes** in PowerShell define **types**.

- **Classes** have **methods** and **behaviors**.

- **Objects** may also have templates, which are called **schemas**.

- Information about objects is referred to as its **members**.

- An example of retrieving **attributes** of an object is **Get-Service | Get-Member -MemberType Property**.

- **Cmdlets** can also be used to retrieve specific properties of objects, such as Get-Service -ServiceName * | Select-Object -Property 'Status'; 'DisplayName', which displays services with two of their properties; DisplayName; and Status.

- It is also possible to format, sort, and measure objects in the output.

- Loops, like **ForEach-Object**, are also useful in looping through the objects retrieved using cmdlets.

Chapter Five: The Pipeline

Pipelines in PowerShell are a series of commands that are connected using the pipeline operators (|). The results of a command from one pipeline operator are sent to the succeeding command. This forms a complex chain of commands in series, also referred to as the pipeline. The general syntax of the pipeline is depicted below:

Command - 1 | Command - 2 | Command - 3

The output of each command is an object, which is sent to the next command. The order of processing of the commands is from left to right, and the output is generated after the processing has been completed for all commands in series. As discussed earlier, commands in PowerShell are cmdlets. An example of a series of cmdlets in PowerShell is included below:

Get-Process notepad | Stop-Process

In the example above, the **Get-Process** cmdlet gets an object of the Notepad process. The | operator is used to send this object to the **Stop-Process** cmdlet. This pipeline may be further extended to include additional functions, such as sorting them and displaying them as a table. The following example demonstrates these additional functions:

Get-ChildItem -Path *.txt | Where-Object {$_.length -gt 10000} | Sort-Object -Property length | Format-Table -Property name, length

The **Get-ChildItem** cmdlet is used to get the files with the .txt extension. These file objects are passed to the **Where-Object** cmdlet, which retrieves the file objects with a length greater than 10000. This output is then passed to the **Sort-Object** cmdlet according to their length. Finally, the output is passed to the **Format-Object** cmdlet that formats the output in the form of a table by their length and name.

Working with Pipeline in PowerShell

In pipelining, the receiving cmdlet must contain a parameter that accepts pipeline input. It is quite simple to find out which parameters of a cmdlet accept pipeline input. To find the parameters of a cmdlet that accept pipeline input, use the **Get-Help** cmdlet with the desired cmdlet and the **-Full** or **-Parameter** options to retrieve the parameters that will accept pipeline input. Examples of this are included below:

Get-Help Start-Service -Full

Get-Help Start-Service -Parameter *

```
PS D:\MyFolder> Get-Help Start-Service -Parameter *

-DisplayName <string[]>
    Specifies the display names of the services to be started. Wildc

    Required?                    true
    Position?                    named
    Default value
    Accept pipeline input?       false
    Accept wildcard characters?  false

-Exclude <string[]>
    Omits the specified services. The value of this parameter qualif
    tern, such as "s*". Wildcards are permitted.

    Required?                    false
    Position?                    named
    Default value
    Accept pipeline input?       false
    Accept wildcard characters?  false
```

When these commands are executed, the output clearly indicates that **-InputObject** and **-Name** are the two parameters, which accept pipeline input.

There are two ways to accept pipeline input - **ByPropertyName** and **ByValue**. When cmdlet parameters accept input by value, it is possible to accept objects that are either strings or those that can be converted into strings. On the other hand, when they accept input by property name, the input object must have a property with the same name as the parameter.

An important aspect of piping is parameter binding. Piping objects from one command to the next allows PowerShell to link piped objects with the parameter linked to the receiving cmdlet. Parameter binding in PowerShell allows the linking of cmdlet parameters with input objects when a certain set of criteria are satisfied: the parameter accepts input from a pipeline, the parameter was not used in the command, and the parameter accepts object type that is sent or the type that can be converted to the expected type of object. This means that even though a certain cmdlet can have a number of parameters, only the **Name** and **InputObject** parameters accept pipeline input.

Parameter binding is an efficient process in PowerShell. It is not possible to forcibly bind a specific parameter in PowerShell. In pipelining, the objects from one cmdlet are piped to the next one, one-at-a time. An example is included below:

Get-Service | Format-Table -Property Name, DependentServices

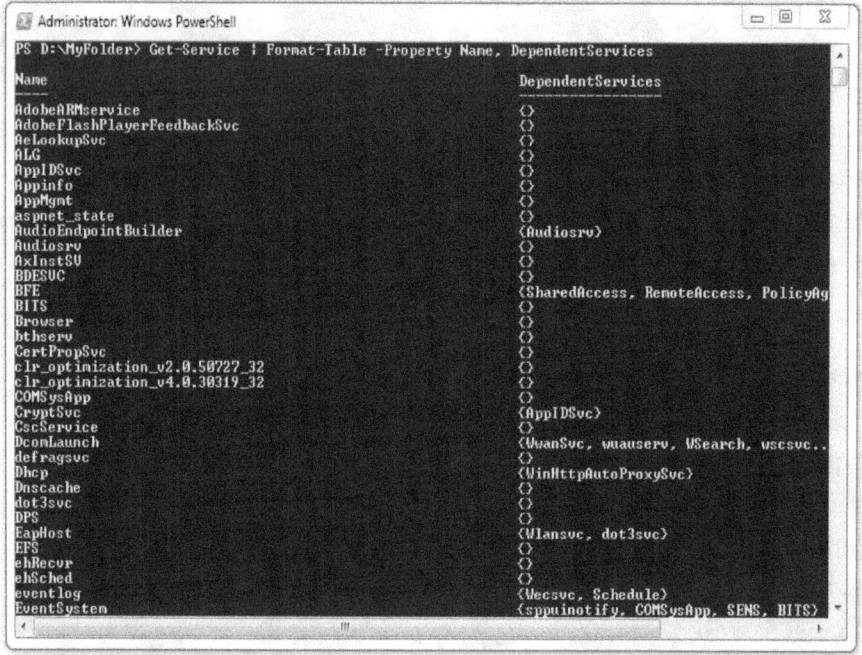

In the example above, the object of the **Get-Service** cmdlet is passed to the **Format-Table** cmdlet, which accepts this object collection. Henceforth, the output which is displayed as a table is sorted according to the **Name** and **DependentServices**. The collection of services available after executing this command is also passed to a variable. This is shown in the command sequence below:

$services = Get-Service

Format-Table -InputObject $services -Property Name, DependentServices

Internally, when PowerShell executes a pipeline, it enumerates any of the types that implement the **IEnumerable** interface. This interface sends members through the pipeline one-at-a-time.

Another common example is when the objects of the **Get-Process** cmdlet are piped into the **Get-Member** cmdlet, which displays the class type of the process objects, along with their methods and properties. This is shown in the example below:

Get-Process | Get-Member

In PowerShell, parameters are bound to the cmdlets using the parameter binding component, which uses specific criteria to achieve this purpose. The first criterion is that the parameter must accept input from a pipeline. The second criterion is that it should accept an object type that is sent or one that can be converted to an accepted type of object. The third criterion is that the parameter was not used as part of the command. A typical example that illustrates this concept is the **Start-Service** cmdlet, which has only two parameters that accept pipeline input. These parameters are **InputObject** and **Name**, which take service objects and strings respectively.

Common Cmdlets Used in Command Pipelines

Most pipelines contain common cmdlets, including **Get-Service, Where-Object, Get-Member, Group-Object, Sort-Object**, and **Measure-Object**. Objects are used with these cmdlets and passed from one cmdlet to another using a pipeline. Other common cmdlets are **Format-List, Format-Table, Export-CSV, Export-Clixml**, and **Out-File**. The examples of these cmdlets are included below:

Cmdlet Pipelines with Get-Service

The **Get-Service** cmdlet returns objects depicting services available on a computer. These services may be running, or they may be those that have been stopped. **Get-Service** takes many parameters, such as **-Displayname, -Name, -RequiredServices** and **-Exclude**. Some examples of using the **Get-Service** cmdlet are included below:

- **Get-Service Spooler | Start-Service** is a series of cmdlets used to invoke the **Spooler** service, whose object is passed to the **Start-Service** cmdlet.

- **Get-Service -Name "win*" -Exclude "WinRM"** gets all services with the name starting with "win" except the WinRM service.

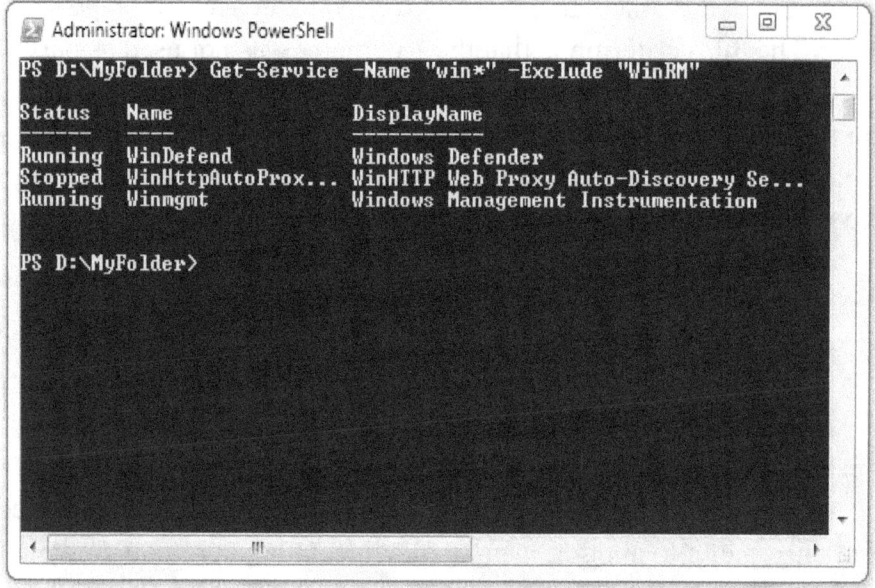

- **Get-Service -Displayname "*network"** displays all services with their name containing the word "network". The same cmdlet can be used to display services that are dependent or those that are currently active.
- The same command can be used to display all services starting with "s" and displaying a sorted list of services. This is achieved by the command pipeline **get-Service "s*" | Sort-Object status**.

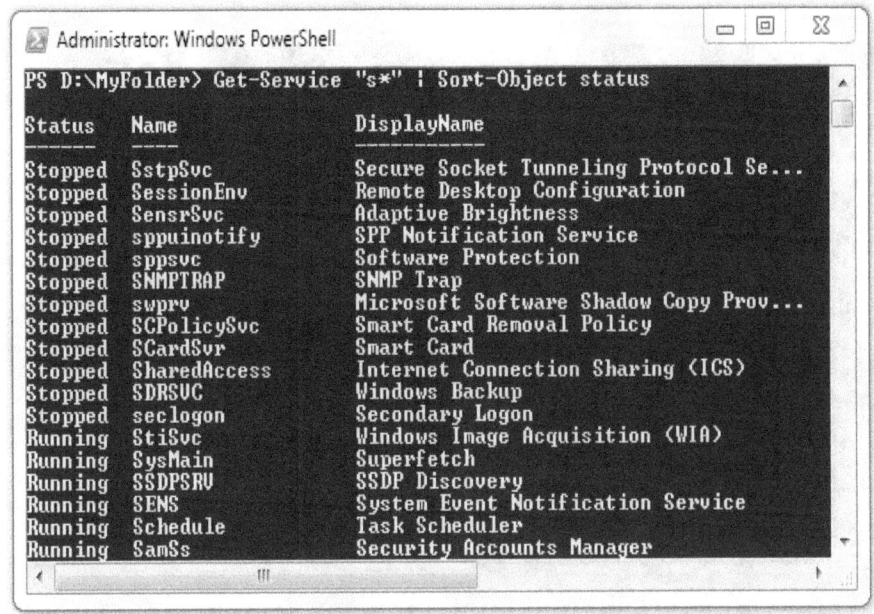

Cmdlet Pipelines with Where-Object

Where-Object cmdlet gets objects with specific property values from a collection of objects. The criteria specified to this cmdlet may pertain to objects with a specific ID, those that were created after a specific date or the ones using a particular version of Windows. The following examples demonstrate the use of the **Where-Object** cmdlet:

- **Get-Process | Where-Object {$_.PriorityClass -eq "Normal"}** the **Where-Object** acts as a filter to get processes in the **Normal** priority by identifying where the value of **PriorityClass** property is **Normal**.

```
Administrator: Windows PowerShell                                    [_][□][X]
PS D:\MyFolder> Get-Process | Where-Object ($_.PriorityClass -eq "Normal")
Handles  NPM(K)    PM(K)     WS(K) VM(M)   CPU(s)     Id ProcessName
   1154      81   199280     25644   377   161.00    168 AcroRd32
    635      19    36812      4716   193     3.48   1432 AcroRd32
     57       3      700       400    31     0.00   1648 armsvc
    181      10    14348     16964   775     1.53   1336 chrome
    184      11    18920     26864   782     7.89   2092 chrome
    177       9    14132      8216   775     0.56   2208 chrome
    192       8    10720      6324   234     4.84   3396 chrome
   1677      43   104312    141492   722   375.28   3692 chrome
    163       4     2352      1704    61     0.59   3716 chrome
    253      12    17628     27340   270   137.98   3888 chrome
    153       7     6176      6636   231     2.03   3916 chrome
    177      11    18344     16836   778     3.00   4072 chrome
    477      42   179632    312220  1238   380.16   4892 chrome
     58       4     1888      6048    49    18.47   2556 conhost
    602       5     1380      1088    33     1.14    372 csrss
    836      12     4916      4308   176    26.06    444 csrss
   1059      37    48876     51212   308    79.48   1556 explorer
    322      30    35520     23956   219    81.22   1140 Feem
    202       7     2672      2032    48     0.16   1708 FlashPlayerFeedba
    110       6     2880      3156    73     0.17    740 GrooveMonitor
     95       6     4476      5268    80    30.80   1780 Lightshot
    742      12     3188      3880    33     7.20    548 lsass
    146       4     1416      1200    14     0.13    556 lsm
    121      24    48032     57100   125    63.88   3656 mspaint
    376      11    54368     51004   197     6.20    352 powershell
```

- Another way to retrieve the objects with a priority **Normal** is **Get-Process | Where-Object -Property PriorityClass -eq -Value "Normal"**. In this example, the command gets the processes that have a priority with the class **Normal**.

- **Get-Service | Where-Object {$_.Status -eq "Stopped"}** gets all services that have stopped by using the **Where-Object** cmdlet and filtering all services with the status "Stopped".

Cmdlet Pipelines with Get-Member

The **Get-Member** cmdlet retrieves the properties and methods of objects. It takes several parameters, including **-name**, **-memberType**, **-inputObject**, and many more. The names of methods and properties of a specific object can be retrieved using the **-name** parameter. It is also possible to specify other criteria using **-View**, **-Static**, or **-MemberType**.

The **Get-Member** cmdlet allows you to find out more about a command by piping the object you want to explore. Information on static members of the class rather than its instance can be retrieved with the **Static** parameter. It is also possible to get only specific members using the **MemberType** parameter.

There are a number of ways you could use to retrieve the list of members with the **Get-Member** cmdlet. To elaborate, **Dynamic** retrieves all dynamic members and **Event** retrieves all events. Further, **PropertySet** retrieves a set of properties and **Properties** retrieves all property member types. Methods and properties defined in scripts can be retrieved using **Scriptmethod** and **Scriptproperty**. **ParameterizedProperty** is another member of the **Get-Member** cmdlet that is neither a method nor a property, but acts like a property that takes parameters.

The following examples demonstrate the use of the **Get-Member** cmdlet:

- **Get-Service | Get-Member Force** is used to retrieve the compiler-generated members and intrinsic members of the objects. The **Get-Member** command when used with the **Force** parameter displays these members.

- Another way to use piping with the **Get-Member** cmdlet is to use the command series **Get-Service | Get-Member -View Extended**. In this example, the **View** parameter of the **Get-Member** cmdlet is used to retrieve the extended members of the objects:

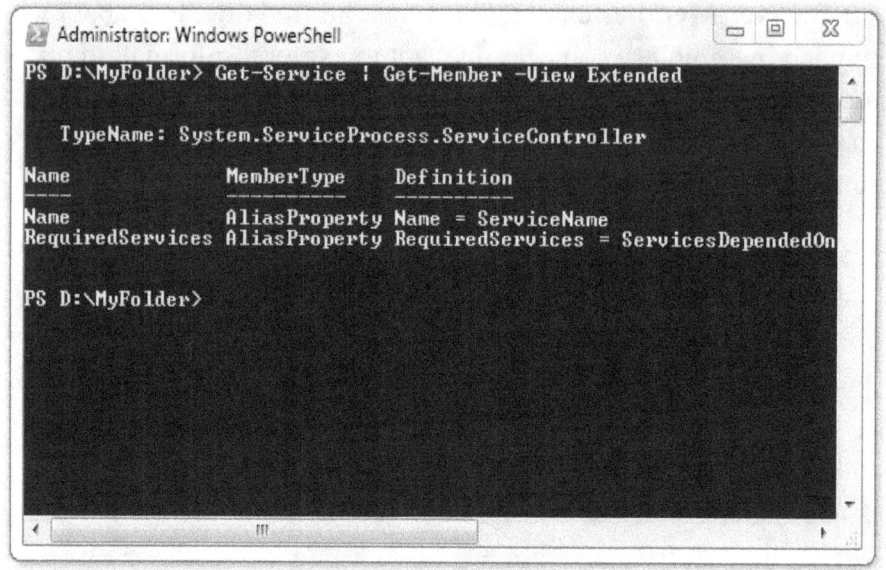

Cmdlet Pipelines with Get-Command

The **Get-Command** cmdlet is a versatile cmdlet that enlists all commands available on the computer, including cmdlets, aliases, workflows, filters, applications, scripts, and functions. Commands that were imported from PowerShell modules and from other sessions are available with **Get-Command**.

The **Get-Command** cmdlet works with a number of arguments, such as **-ListImported**, **-ParameterName**, **-ParameterType**, **-Module**, **-Name**, **-Noun**, and many more. Some examples of using the **Get-Command** cmdlet are included below:

- **Get-Command *** retrieves all functions, aliases, filters, and cmdlets.
- Sending the output of **Get-Command** to **Get-Member** retrieves all properties and methods.
- To get the syntax of a specific cmdlet in PowerShell, the **Get-Command Get-Process -Syntax** may be used.

- **Get-Command -CommandType Cmdlet** retrieves all cmdlets, and **Get-Command -CommandType Alias** retrieves only the aliases in PowerShell.

It is possible to use these and other cmdlets to send the objects available from one cmdlet to another cmdlet through a command pipeline.

- **Get-Command dir | Format-List *** can be used to retrieve the object for the **dir**, and the output is routed to **Format-List ***, which makes all properties available.

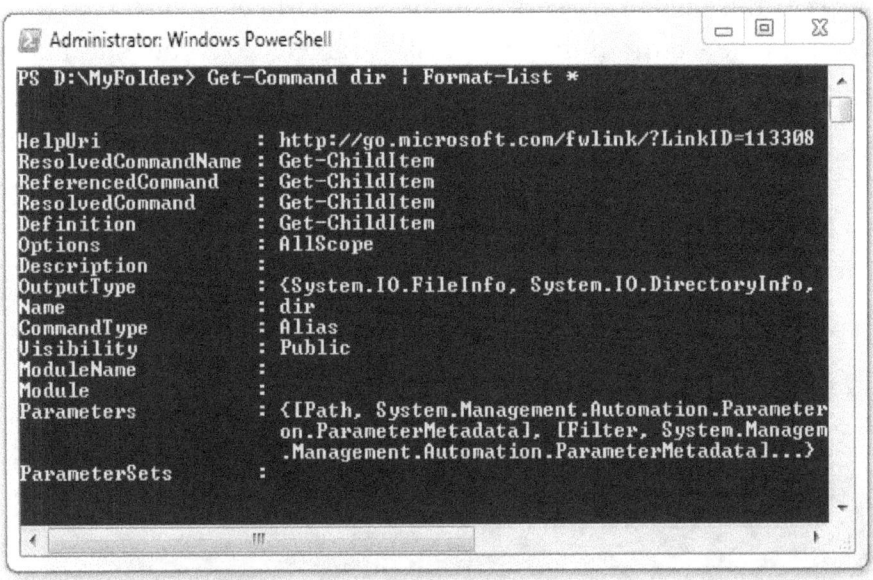

- All cmdlets that have a specific output type can be retrieved using the **Get-Command -Type Cmdlet | Where-Object OutputType | Format-List -Property Name, OutputType**. This cmdlet pipeline gives output in the form of name and output type pairs by passing all cmdlets through the **Where-Object** filter to retrieve them according to their output type and finally format the output according to the property name and output type.

Cmdlet Pipelines with Group-Object

The **Group-Object** cmdlet groups objects containing the same value for the parameters specified. The output is in the form of a table containing a column for the property value and the number of items with that value. In the example illustrated below, the **Get-ChildItem** cmdlet is called with the **-Path** parameter, which takes the desired path along with the **-Recurse** parameter. The object returned by this cmdlet is passed to the **Group-Object** cmdlet by specifying the parameter **-Property** as **extension**. The **-NoElement** parameter does not display the members of the group as part of the output. The objects of this cmdlet are passed to the **Sort-Object** cmdlet, which uses the value **Count** of the **-Property** parameter to sort the results in the descending order.

$files = Get-ChildItem -Path $PSHOME -Recurse

$files | Group-Object -Property extension -NoElement | Sort-Object -Property Count -Descending

```
Windows PowerShell
PS C:\Users\ss> $files = Get-ChildItem -Path $PSHOME -Recurse
PS C:\Users\ss> $files | Group-Object -Property extension -NoElement | Sort-Object -Property Count -Descending

Count Name
   91 .txt
   13 .ps1xml
   10
   10 .xml
    7 .dll
    5 .psd1
    4 .mui
    2 .exe
    1 .psm1
    1 .ps1

PS C:\Users\ss>
```

Another example of the **Group-Object** cmdlet uses the **Property** parameter to display the odd and even numbers using the pipeline syntax shown below:

1..40 | Group-Object -Property {$_ % 2}

```
PS C:\Users\ss> 1..40 | Group-Object -Property {$_ %2}

Count Name                      Group
----- ----                      -----
   20 1                         {1, 3, 5, 7...}
   20 0                         {2, 4, 6, 8...}

PS C:\Users\ss>
```

In the example above, the numbers from 1-40 are supplied to the **Group-Object** cmdlet, and the **Property** parameter is used to generate the list of odd and even numbers.

To group the different events in the event log, the events on the system can be passed to the **Group-Object** cmdlet. The following cmdlet pipeline displays the number of events in each log (count), followed by the type of event that define a group (name), and the objects in each group (group):

Get-WinEvent -LogName System -MaxEvents 1000 | Group-Object -Property LevelDisplayName

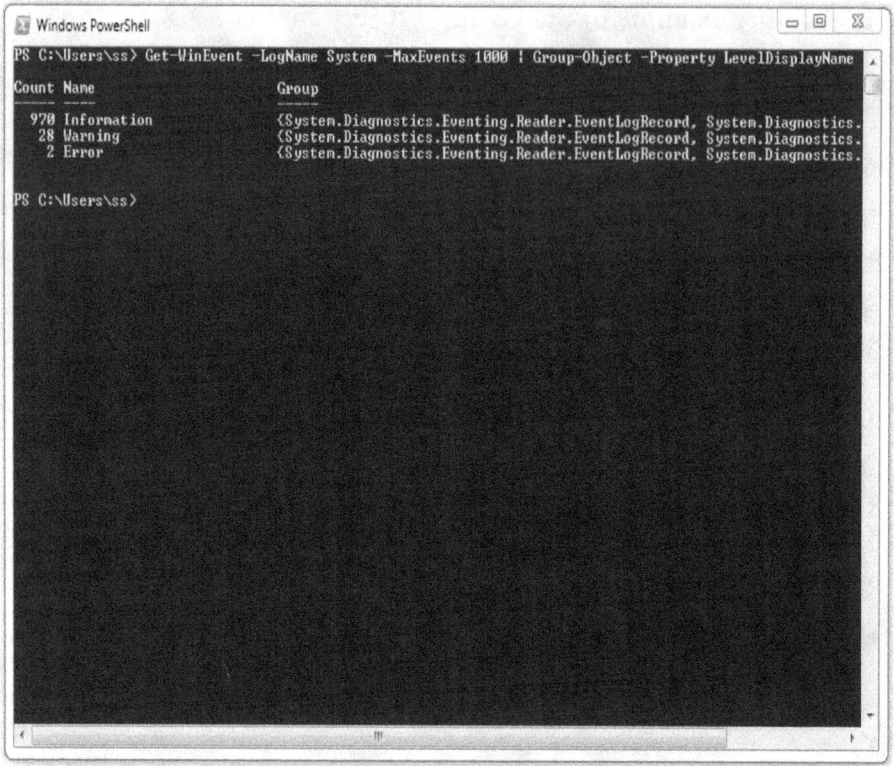

In a similar manner, processes can also be grouped in several ways as indicated below:

- **Get-Process | Group-Object -Property PriorityClass** takes all processes from the **Get-Process** cmdlet and passes them to the **Group-Object** cmdlet to be grouped by the **PriorityClass** property.

- The **Group-Object** cmdlet can be used in another way by specifying **Get-Process | Group-Object -Property PriorityClass -NoElement**, which eliminates the members of the group from the output. The result is displayed only with the output of the **Name** and **Count** properties.

- The **Group-Object** cmdlet can also be used with the **Where-Object** cmdlet by specifying **Get-Process | Group-Object -**

Property Name -NoElement | Where-Object {$_.Count -gt 1}. Executing this cmdlet pipeline provides the processes available from the **Get-Process** cmdlet to the **Group-Object** cmdlet, which groups the objects in a specific manner then passes this output to the **Where-Object** cmdlet, which has the desired criteria.

Cmdlet Pipelines with Sort-Object

The **Sort-Object** cmdlet is used to sort objects in the ascending and descending order based on property values of the object. When a command does not have sort properties, PowerShell uses the sort properties belonging to the first input object. When no sort properties are available, PowerShell compares the objects.

It is possible to sort objects using a single property or multiple properties. When multiple properties are specified for sorting objects, PowerShell uses hash tables to perform the sorting in descending order, ascending order, or a combination of sort orders. Properties can be sorted according to case sensitivity and by using the **Unique** parameter that eliminates duplicates. The following examples demonstrate the use of the **Sort-Object** cmdlet:

- A simple use of the **Sort-Object** cmdlet is to see the processes that are consuming most of the CPU time by passing the objects of the **Get-Process** to the **Sort-Object** cmdlet.

    The command is specified as **Get-Process | Sort-Object -Property CPU**

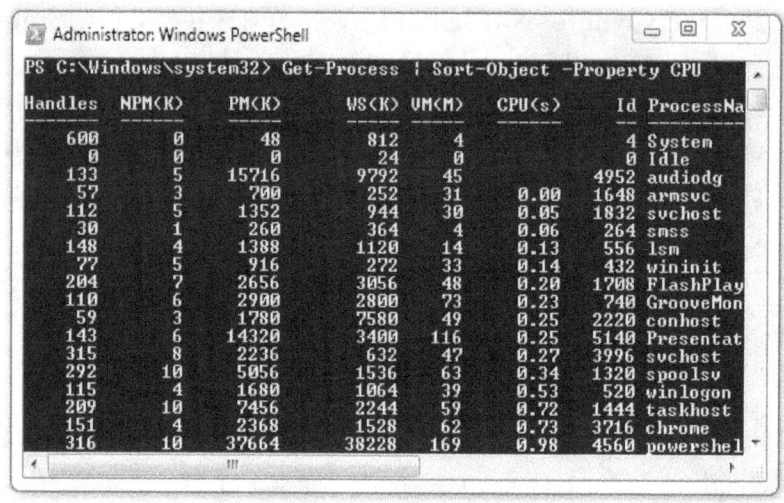

It is also possible to sort the objects by not just CPU usage but also by the name of the process by specifying the cmdlet pipeline as indicated below:

Get-Process | Sort-Object -Property CPU, ProcessName

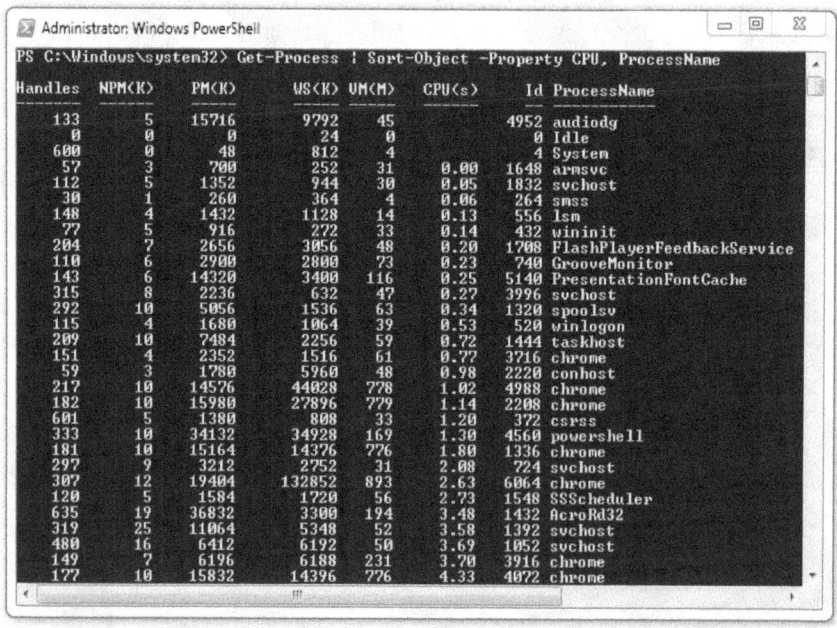

The output from this command pipeline can be further fine-tuned to select specific columns, such as the pipeline indicated below:

Get-Process | Sort-Object -Property CPU -Descending | Select-Object ProcessName, CPU

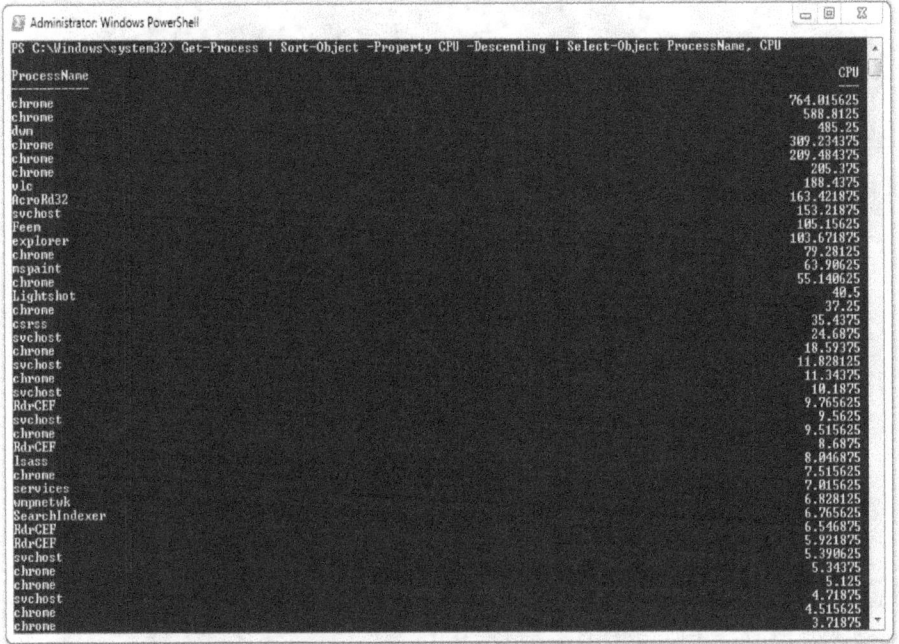

Additional filters can be applied using the **Where-Object** cmdlet as shown below:

Get-Process | Where-Object {$_.CPU -gt 10} | Sort-Object -Property CPU -Descending | Select-Object ProcessName, CPU

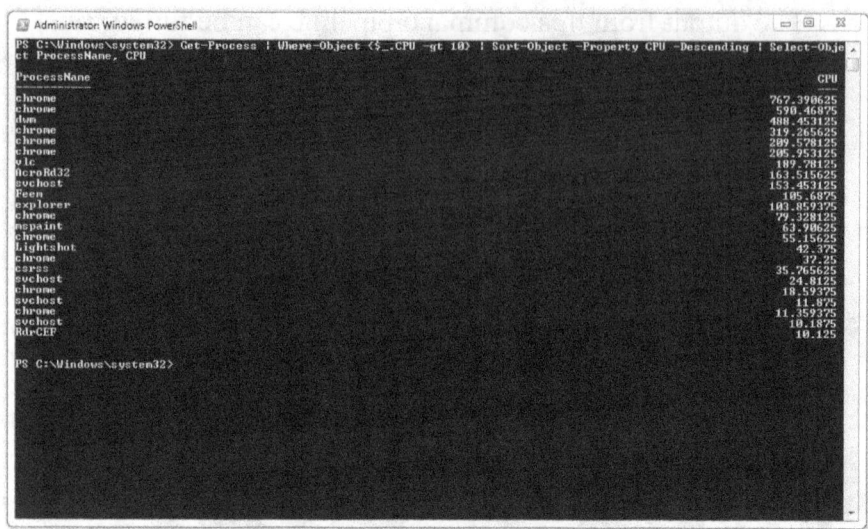

The following cmdlet pipeline displays only the first ten rows of the output sorted in descending order as shown below:

Get-Process | Sort-Object -Property CPU -Descending | Select-Object ProcessName, CPU -First 10

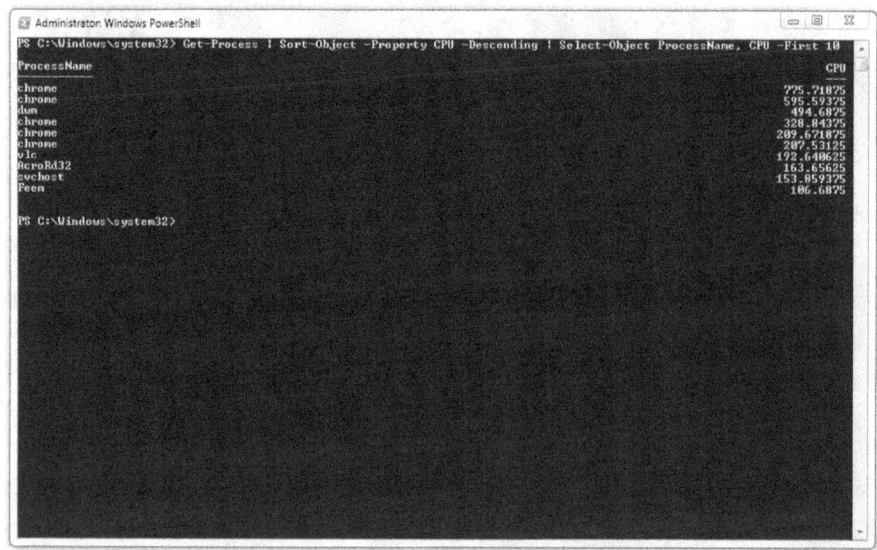

- To get all the files and the subdirectories specified by a path, and then sort the objects according to the default criteria, use the pipeline shown below:

    Get-ChildItem -Path D:\MyFolder | Sort-Object.

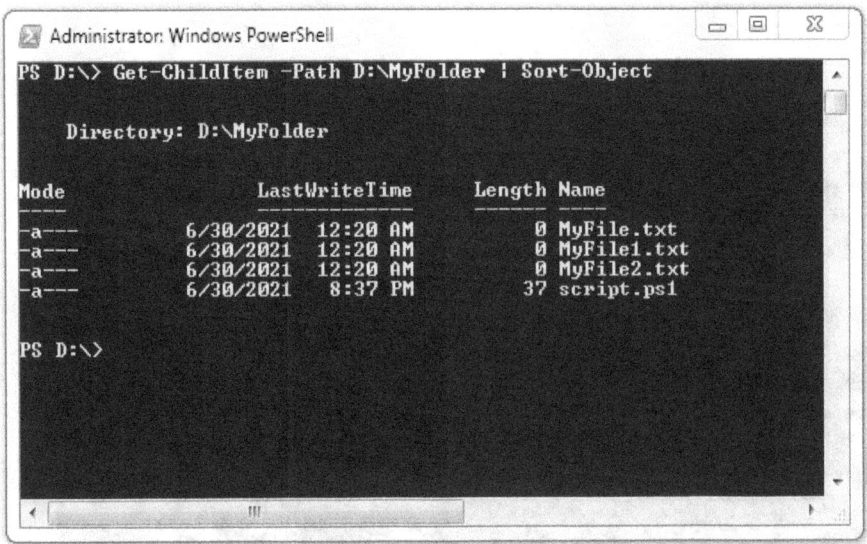

    The **Get-ChildItem** first retrieves all files and directories from the path "D:\MyDirectory". These objects are sent to the **Sort-Object** cmdlet. In the final output, the files are sorted by name.

- It is also possible to sort the files in the current directory by their name using the following cmdlet pipeline:

    Get-ChildItem -Path C:\Test -File | Sort-Object -Property Length

    The name of the file and its length are included in the output along with other parameters, such as the time when the file was last written.

- Memory usage is another frequently used parameter to sort objects in PowerShell. The following example demonstrated the use of memory, referred to as working set and abbreviated as WS to sort the processes:

Get-Process | Sort-Object -Property WS | Select-Object -Last 5

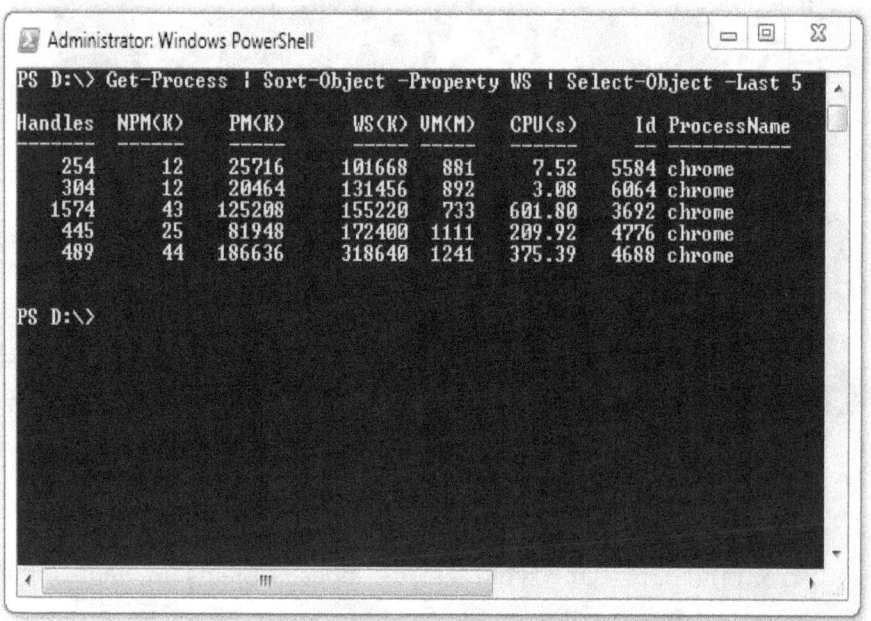

In this example, the **Get-Process** retrieves all processes running on the system. These objects are passed to the **Sort-Object** cmdlet, which uses the working set (WS) to perform the sorting. Finally, this output is sent to the **Select-Object** cmdlet, which displays the last five objects using the **Last** property. These are the objects with the highest memory usage.

- Further, lists in text files can also be sorted with the **Sort-Object** cmdlet. The cmdlet pipeline for displaying all files in a list is:

Get-Content -Path D:\MyFile.txt displays all files in a list.

To sort the files in alphabetical order, the cmdlet pipeline used is:

Get-Content -Path D:\MyFile.txt | Sort-Object.

Finally, unique items in the list can be displayed using the pipeline:

Get-Content -Path D:\MyFile.txt | Sort-Object -Unique

- **Sort-Object** is a versatile cmdlet and can also be used to sort integers in a text file. To perform this operation, the following cmdlet pipeline may be used:

Get-Content -Path D:\MyDocument.txt | Sort-Object sorts the contents as strings. The same cmdlet can be used to sort them as integers by specifying the sort criteria as **{[int]$_}**:

Get-Content -Path D:\MyDocument.txt | Sort-Object {[int]$_}

- Properties can also be sorted in the ascending or descending order using a hash table. In the following example, the **Get-Service** cmdlet retrieves all services. This object is passed to the **Sort-Object** cmdlet, and the sorting is performed using the parameter **Property**. The services are first sorted according to their status in the descending order, such that the running services are displayed before the stopped services. Further, the services in each group are sorted in the ascending alphabetical order as displayed in the cmdlet pipeline below:

Get-Service | Sort-Object -Property @{Expression = "Status"; Descending = $True}, @{Expression = "DisplayName"; Descending = $False}

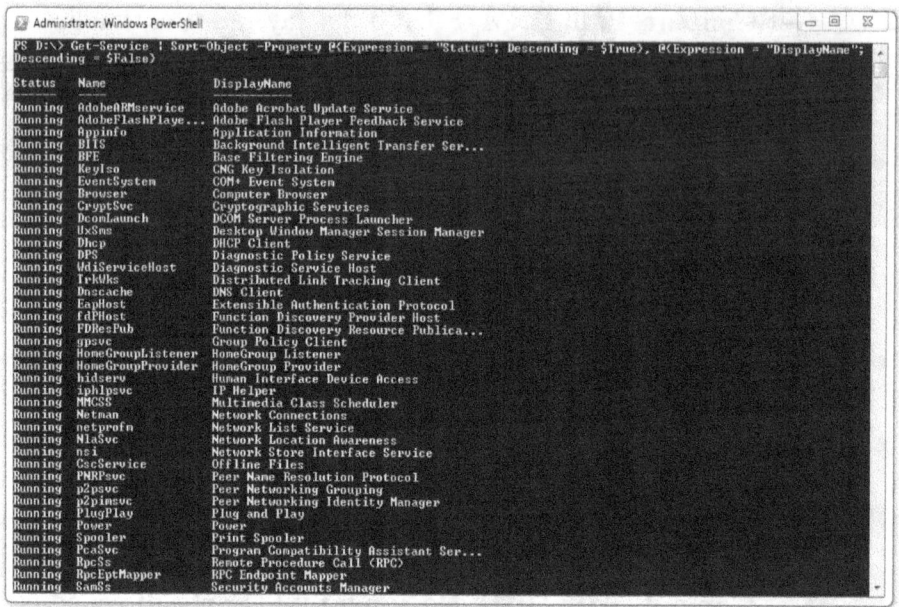

Cmdlet Pipelines with Measure-Object

Measure-Object is a versatile cmdlet used for properties, such as lines, words, and characters in string objects, and other numeric properties of objects. A number of the numeric properties of objects can be calculated using the **Measure-Object** cmdlet, like the sum, minimum value, maximum value, average, and standard deviation. Some common examples of **Measure-Object** are included below:

- The simplest way to use **Measure-Object** is to get the number of objects supplied to it in a cmdlet pipeline, such as **0..15 | Measure-Object**

The same example can be extended to obtain more numerical measurements by supplying additional parameters, like the example specified below:

0..15 | Measure-Object -Sum -Average -Maximum - Minimum

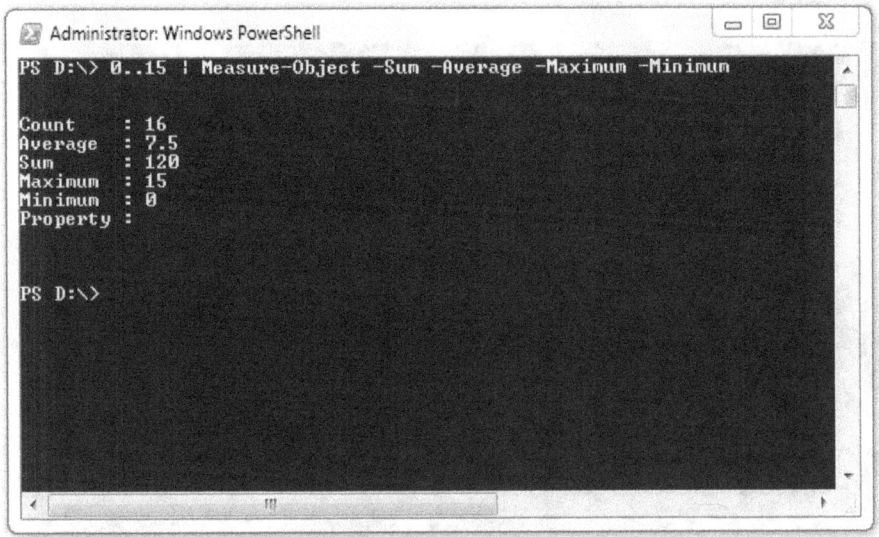

The information obtained from the above cmdlet pipeline is sum, average, maximum, and minimum of the numbers supplied.

- The cmdlet pipeline **Get-ChildItem | Measure-Object -Property length-Minimum -Maximum -Average** displays the sizes of files in the current directory along with the average file size in the directory.
- Simply executing **Get-ChildItem | Measure-Object** displays the number of files and directories in the current directory.
- It is also possible to get the complete information about characters, words, and lines by storing and retrieving the content in a text file using the **Set-Content** and **Get-Content** cmdlets. The following cmdlet pipeline can be used to store content in a file, and then retrieve the content to measure the numerical aspects of the content:

"This", "dog", "has", "a", "tail" | Set-Content -Path C:\MyFile.txt Get-Content C:\MyFile.txt | Measure-Object -Line -Word - Character

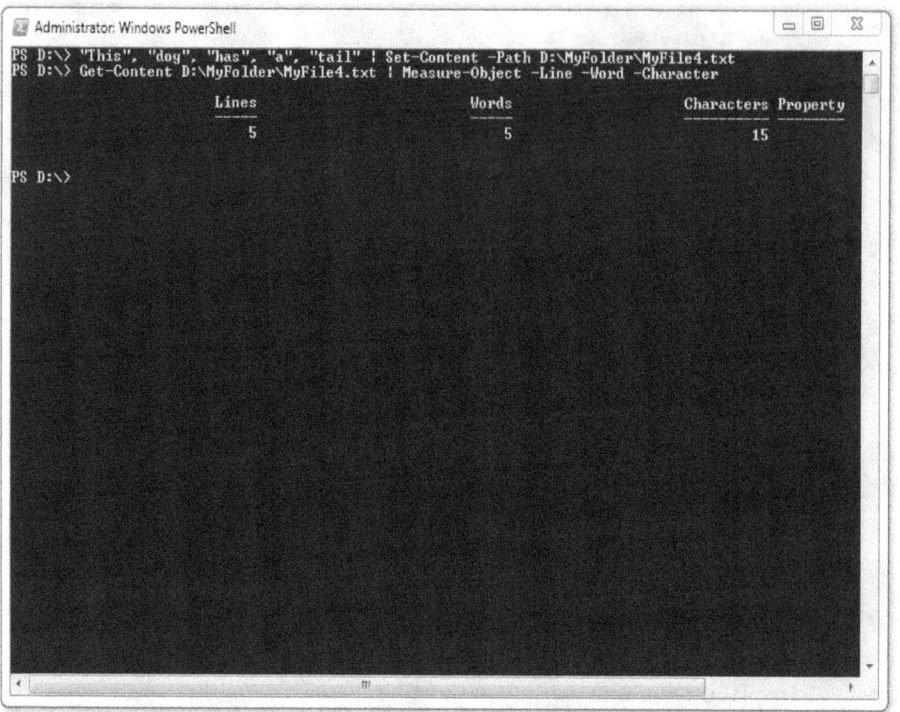

This cmdlet pipeline displays columns for lines, words, and characters so that the output shows 5 lines, 5 words, and 15 characters as the numerical indicators of the text supplied to the file.

- The **Measure-Object** cmdlet can also be used to measure the services and processes on a system. It can also be used to measure objects that have a specific property.

To display a count of all processes, the cmdlet pipeline **Get-Service | Measure-Object** may be used. Further, the processes may be measured using the cmdlet pipeline **Get-Process | Measure-Object** pipeline. Alternatively, the processes and services can be stored in a variable and collectively piped to the **Measure-Object** cmdlet to get the total count as shown below:

$services = Get-Service

$processes = Get-Process

$services + $processes | Measure-Object

```
Administrator: Windows PowerShell
PS D:\> $services = Get-Service
PS D:\> $Processes = Get-Process
PS D:\> $Services + $Processes | Measure-Object

Count    : 227
Average  :
Sum      :
Maximum  :
Minimum  :
Property :


PS D:\>
```

The **Measure-Object** cmdlet can be used to get a number of different measurements, including hash tables, scriptblock properties, wild cards, and standard deviation. It takes a number of parameters including **-Average**, which gets the average of the properties indicated, **-Character**, which counts the characters in the objects supplied as input, **-AllStats**, which displays all statistics pertaining to a property, **-Line**, which counts the number of lines in an input object, and the **-Maximum** and **-Minimum**, which show the maximum and minimum values of the properties respectively. Other frequently used parameters are the **-Sum** to display the sum of values of a specific property and **-Word**, which indicates the number of words in input objects.

Cmdlet Pipelines with Out-File

It is possible to send output to a file using the **Out-File** cmdlet. The following examples demonstrate the use of **Out-File** cmdlet:

- The **Out-File** cmdlet can be used simply to append content to the end of a text file. In order to perform this operation, simply pass the content to the **Out-File** cmdlet in a pipeline. The command pipeline used to perform this is indicated below:

'test' | **Out-File -FilePath D:\Test.txt**

The command above writes the supplied text content to the file specified in the path. The content of the file is overwritten with this supplied content. To append the contents of the file without overwriting the existing content, the **-Append** parameter may be added to the pipeline as shown below:

'test' | **Out-File -FilePath D:\Test.txt -Append**

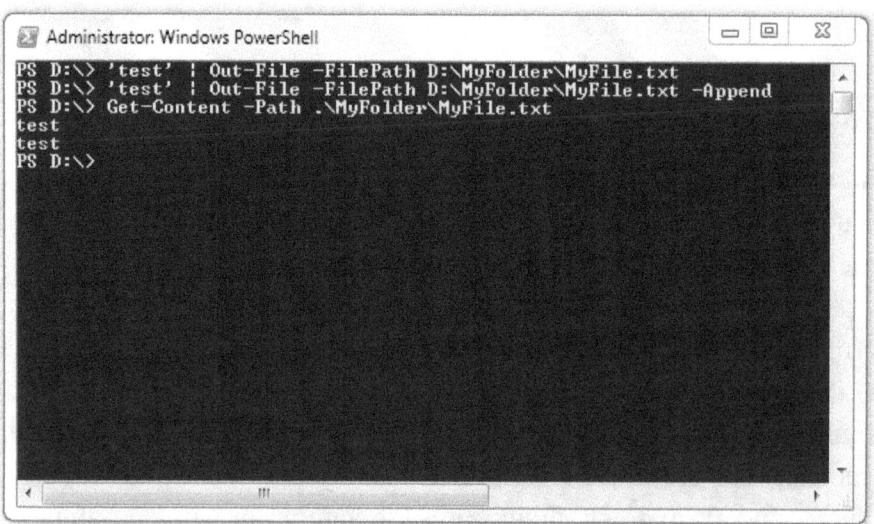

- **Get-Process | Out-File -FilePath D:\Processes.txt -NoClobber** writes all processes running on the computer to the file path specified. The **-NoClobber** parameter is added to specify that the file should not be overwritten.

- To specify output format for the target file, the **-Encoding** parameter may be used, and ASCII may be specified as the desired encoding.

$Procs = Get-Process

Out-File -FilePath D:\Processes.txt -InputObject $Procs -Encoding ASCII -Width 100

The **Get-Process** cmdlet retrieves all processes and stores it in the **$Procs** variable. Finally, the **Out-File** cmdlet is used along with the path of the file specified by **-FilePath** parameter.

- In a similar manner, the services can be routed to a different file using the cmdlet pipeline **Get-Service | Out-File -FilePath D:\MyServices.txt**

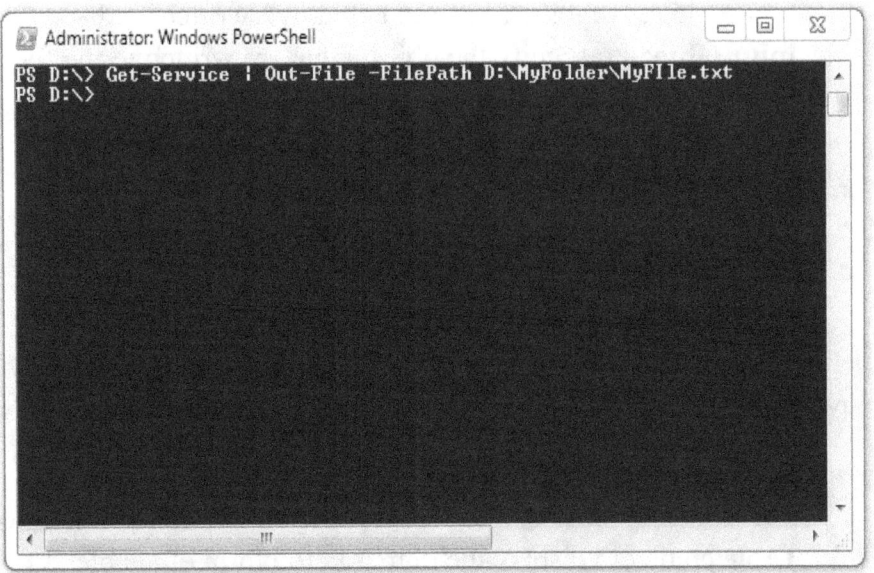

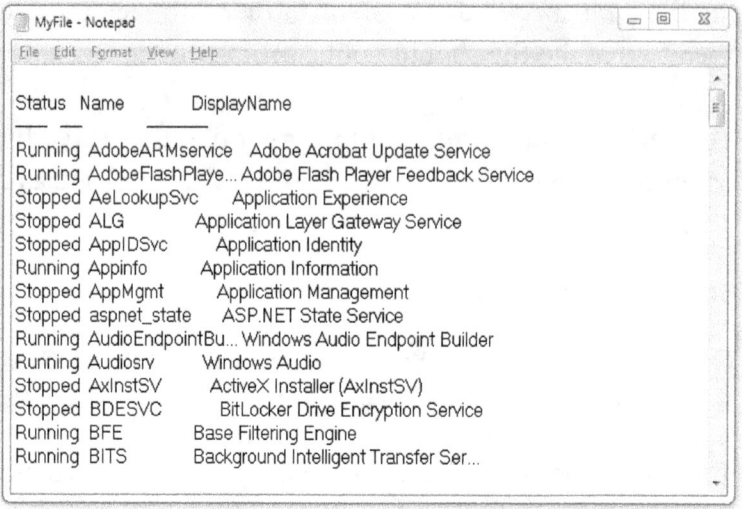

In line with the parameters shown above, **Out-File** takes a number of parameters, such as **-LiteralPath** and **-FilePath** to specify the path to the file, **-Append** to append the contents at the end of the output, **-Force** to overwrite existing read-only attributes and files, **-NoCobbler** to detect if a file already exists and prevent the file from being overwritten, and **-InputObject** to specify the objects that are written to the file. Specifying the **-Confirm** parameter asks you for a confirmation before a cmdlet is executed, and **-WhatIf** describes the expected outcome if the cmdlet is executed.

Cmdlet Pipelines with Format-Table

The **Format-Table** cmdlet displays formatted output in a pipeline. There are several ways the output can be formatted as shown below:

- Giving **Get-Host | Format-Table -Autosize** gets the objects that represent the host and passes these objects to the **Format-Table** cmdlet to display the output in the form of a table. Column width is adjusted by using the **-Autosize** parameter to prevent the truncation of the output.

- Several other cmdlets can be used to filter and sort the output, such as sorting processes and displaying them as a table:

Get-Process | Sort-Object StartTime | Format-Table -View StartTime

This cmdlet pipeline first gets all processes then passes those objects to the **Sort-Object** cmdlet with the **StartTime** parameter. This allows the objects to be sorted according to their start date. These objects are passed to the **Format-Table** cmdlet, which formats the output then displays it. The output is displayed to show the start date.

- Another way to process the output is to retrieve the processes and sort and display them by using a specific grouping. An example of the cmdlet pipeline is shown below:

Get-Process | Sort-Object -Property BasePriority | Format-Table -GroupBy BasePriority -Wrap

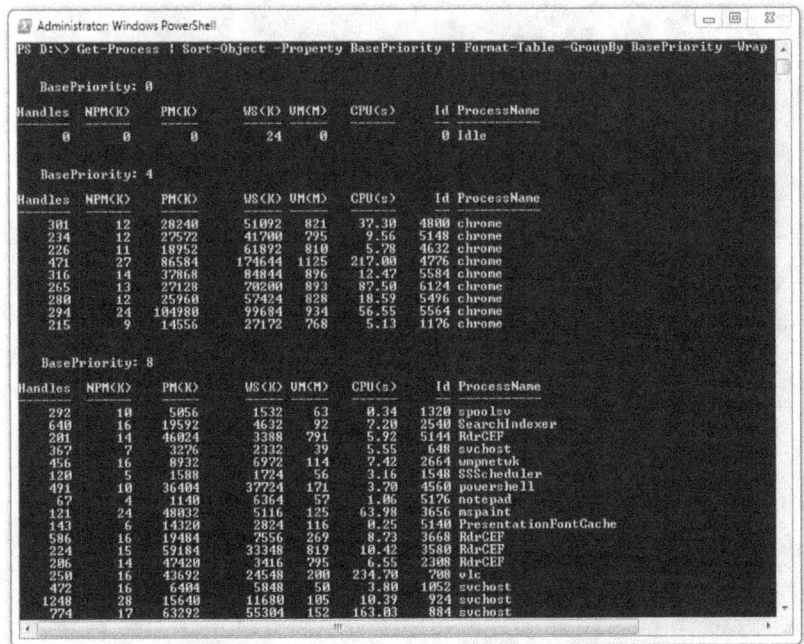

In the example above, the processes are retrieved using the **Get-Process** cmdlet and passing to the **Sort-Object** cmdlet by specifying that they must be sorted according to the property, **BasePriority**. This output is then passed to the **Format-Table** cmdlet, and the objects are grouped by **BasePriority**. An additional parameter **Wrap** is specified to indicate that the data should not be truncated.

- As indicated in the examples in the preceding sections, there are several ways to format the table displaying the output using its properties, such as **Name** and **DependentServices**:

Get-Service | Format-Table -Property Name, DependentServices

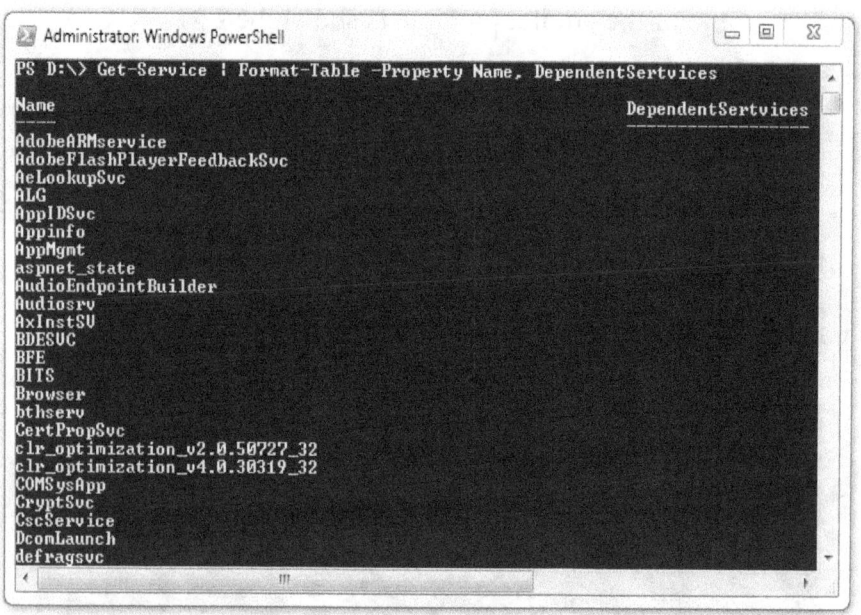

The **Format-Table** cmdlet can use several parameters, such as **-DisplayError** to display errors on the command line, **-Autosize** to automatically adjust column size based on the width of the data, **-Force** to forcibly display all error information, **-GroupBy** to group objects in a specific format, such as using its name or a specific expression. The **-Property** parameter specifies object properties along with the order in which they are displayed.

In effect, the output from one or multiple cmdlets can be displayed in multiple formats using the **format-list** and **format-table** cmdlets. At the most basic level, cmdlets, like **Write-Output**, allow you to write output on the PowerShell console. Other tasks performed by pipelining objects are based on services in PowerShell, such as **Get-Service** and **Restart-Service**. Pipelines in PowerShell are efficient tools to restart a specific service (**Get-Service -Name seclogon | Restart-Service**) and stopping a service (**Get-Service -Name seclogon | Restart-Service -PassThru | Stop-Service**). In effect, the PowerShell pipeline can be used to perform powerful operations by passing objects to different cmdlets and leveraging their potential in the best possible manner.

Chapter Summary

- Series of commands are referred to as pipelines in PowerShell.

- The pipe operator (|) is used to connect different cmdlets in PowerShell to form pipelines.

- The basic syntax of a pipeline is **Command - 1 | Command - 2 | Command - 3**.

- An example of a pipeline that accesses the "notepad" process and attempts to stop it is demonstrated using the pipeline **Get-Process notepad | Stop-Process**.

- The **Format-Table** cmdlet is often used to format the output from cmdlet pipelines.
- Other popular constructions of PowerShell pipelines include **Get-Process | Get-Member**.

- The **Get-Service** cmdlet is also used frequently in pipelines, as in the case of **Get-Service Spooler | Start-Service**, which starts the Spooler service.

- The Where-Object is a common filter applied to cmdlet pipelines. An example that demonstrates retrieving all services with the "stopped" status is **Get-Service | Where-Object {$_.Status -eq "Stopped"}**.

- Cmdlet pipelines can also be constructed using **Get-Member**, as in the case of **Get-Service | Get-Member -View Extended**, which retrieves extended members of the objects.

- Other common cmdlets used in pipelines include **Get-Command, Group-Object, Measure-Object, Sort-Object,** and **Out-File**.

Chapter Six: Scripting in PowerShell

Powerful scripting is possible with PowerShell due to its range of features, including task-oriented design that supports command-line tools and existing scripts and cmdlets, which make it possible to perform administrative tasks while giving enough flexibility to manage processes, services, registry, and event logs. Further, scripting allows you to manage tasks through existing command line tools and scripts. It provides a consistent syntax and design with data sharing through an interface that allows pipelining objects from one cmdlet to another.

The flexible and extensive capabilities of PowerShell are available because of its object-oriented interface that provides a set of tools with the required manipulation capabilities. Moreover, its interface is extensible and customizable, which means that it allows enterprise developers and vendors to use utilities and tools that can be used with PowerShell. The most important features of PowerShell, which makes it possible to execute simple as well as complex scripts are described below:

- Variables: Variables can be easily created in PowerShell using the $ preceding the variable name. Variables are useful in manipulating objects. A variable name in PowerShell can have alphanumeric characters as well as the underscore sign. An example of creating a variable by assigning a location to it is given below:

    $variable_location = Get-Location

    This script contains a variable with the name "variable_location", which takes the object of the cmdlet **Get-Location**. The **Get-Location** cmdlet gets the reference to the current location.

It is also possible to declare arrays as variables and work with them. Arrays contain sequential elements of a specific data type. An array may contain either variables or objects as part of its collection. The advantage of using arrays is to be able to refer to the entire collection with a single name while identifying the different elements of the array using sequential indexes. An array is also declared using a $ sign preceding the variable name as shown below:

$Array_Test = 2, 4, 6, 8

PowerShell also allows several operations on arrays, including getting the length of the array, retrieving a specific portion of the array, assigning values to array elements, and traversing through the array using loops.

In addition, it is also possible to declare hashtable variables in the form of pairs of keys and values. An example of declaring a hashtable variable is indicated below:

$hash = @{ Number = 1; Color = "Red"}

Another variable type that can be created using PowerShell is the ordered dictionary, which is used to maintain the order of the elements defined in it, unlike the hashtable that does not maintain the order. An example indicating the definition of an ordered dictionary is defined below:

$hash = [ordered]@{ Number = 1; Color = "Blue"}

The keys and values in a hashtable are accessible using the dot notation (.), such as **$hash.keys** or **$hash.values**. In the example above, the notation **$hash.keys** refers to "number" and "color" while **$hash.values** refers to "1" and "red".

- Automatic Variables: PowerShell uses automatic variables to store specific information. For example, the current object is stored in a variable with the **$_** operator, **$^** representing the first token from the last line in the session. Further, the execution status of the last operation is represented by the **$?** operator. It contains either a TRUE or FALSE value depending on the status of the last operation. Finally, the **$$** operator is used to indicate the last token of the last line that the session receives. PowerShell features several other operators, such as **$ERROR** representing an error object array with the most recent errors, **$EXECUTIONCONTEXT** representing the context of execution according to the PowerShell engine, **$HOME** representing the full home directory path, **$PROFILE** representing the full path of the PowerShell profile including the user, application, and host. The **$SENDER** object refers to the object that generated the event. Finally, PowerShell also has the **$TRUE** and **$FALSE** variables, which represent **TRUE** and **FALSE** respectively.

- Arrays: The **@** symbol is used to convert lists into arrays. For example, an array may be defined as **$var_arr = @{name=** "svchost", "explorer"} where the variable **$var_arr** holds the contents of the array defined using the **@** symbol. The array consists of two process names, **svchost** and **explorer**. To display all processes used by both **svchost** and **explorer**, the **Get-Process** cmdlet may simply be used to get all processes used by them. Executing the cmdlet **Get-Process @procs** achieves this outcome.

- Operators: PowerShell has operators, like comparison operators, arithmetic operators, logical operators, redirectional operators, unary operators, and many more, to carry out different operations. Arithmetic operators are used to perform basic functions, such as addition (**+**), subtraction (**-**), division (**/**), multiplication (*****), and modulus (**%**). Similar to any other scripting language, PowerShell also features the comparison operators, including greater than (>), equal to (=), and lesser than (<), and combinations of these basic operators. In addition, PowerShell has assignment operators, including = (equal to), += (), and (-=) to perform assignment operations, and the assignment operators **NOT**, **AND**, and **OR** to perform the logical operations.

- Split and Join Operators: The **split** operator is a special type of operator that may be used to break a sentence into a number of parts separated by a specific character, such as a whitespace. For example, specifying **"This is a sentence" -split " "** tells PowerShell to split the sentence wherever there is a space. This means that the output is displayed in the form of one-word-per-line format. Likewise, the **join** operator tells PowerShell to join two words or strings using the character specified at the end of the command definition. For example, specifying **"Cat", "the", "mat" -join " "** tells PowerShell to join the words **cat**, **the**, and **mat** using a space between them, as indicated by the **join** operator.

- Backtick Operator: The backtick operator is an important operator in PowerShell that is essentially used in word-wrapping the command syntax. The use of the backtick operator allows commands to span multiple lines. The backtick operator is also used in the definition of a tab space (`t) and newline (`n). For example, the command **Write-host "Firstname `tLastname"** writes **Firstname** and **Lastname** separated by a tab space. Similarly, the two words can be separated by a new line by specifying **Write-host "Firstname `nLastname"**.

- Decision Making: PowerShell provides decision-making capabilities using the **if** statement (boolean expression followed by some statements), **if...else** (a boolean statement that must be tested true for the **if** block to be executed, and **false** for the statements in the **else** block to be executed), nested **if** (using multiple **if** and **else** statements inside the blocks), and **switch** (to test a variable against a list of different values) statements.

- Looping: PowerShell uses looping to execute statement sequentially for a specific number of times. The loop executes as long as the condition specified in the code is satisfied. Conditions are usually specified in the **if...else** conditional block. The different types of loops offered by PowerShell include a while loop, which repeats a set of statements as long as the given statement is true. The specified condition is tested each time before the body of the loop is executed. The **do...while** loop is similar to the **while** loop except that the condition specified for continuing the loop is tested at the end of the set of statements instead of testing them at the beginning of the loop. Furthermore, the **for** loop also executes a sequence of statements sequentially multiple times by specifying the condition at the beginning of the loop. Finally, the **foreach** loop is similar to the **for** loop and can be used to manipulate arrays.

- Regular Expressions: A regular expression is a character sequence used to find other strings by using a specialized syntax pattern. For example, the $ matches the end of the line and **re+** one or more of the previous things. The expression to match word characters is \w and one that matches nonword characters is \W. Similarly, \s matches whitespace and \S matches non-whitespace.

- Conditional Statements: Decision-making is an important aspect of PowerShell. The conditions to be evaluated are supplied to the decision-making structure. In addition, the statements to be executed when the condition is tested true or false are also specified in the conditional statement structure. In PowerShell, there are several types of decision-making structures, such as the **if** statement (boolean expression followed by one or more statements), **if ... else** statement (a boolean expression that executes a set of statements when it is true, and another statement or set of statements that execute when the condition is false), **switch** statement (allows a variable to be tested for equality, and this test is done against a list of given values), and the **nested if** statement.

File and Folder Operations

PowerShell allows the execution of a number of commands related to the creation of files and folders and specific operations on them. These examples are included below:

- To create a new folder, use the following cmdlet:

    New-Item -Path 'D:\MyFolder' -ItemType Directory.

    This creates a folder by the name **MyFolder** under the **D** drive.

- The following cmdlet creates a file with the name **MyFile.txt** under the folder **MyFolder**:

    New-Item -Path 'D:\MyFolder MyFile.txt' -ItemType File.

- It is also possible to copy a folder and save it to a different location with a new name. The following cmdlet copies a folder by the name **MyFolder** and saves it to the target location with the name **MyFolder2**:

    Copy-Item 'D:\Folders MyFolder' 'D:\Folders MyFolder1'

- The **Copy-Item** cmdlet can also be used to copy files from one location to another. The following example demonstrates how to copy files from one location to another:

Copy-Item 'D:\MyFolder MyFile.txt' 'D:\MyFolder MyFile1.txt'

Likewise, several operations can be carried out on files and directories to achieve the desired result. **Remove-Item** can be used to delete a directory or a file, **Move-Item** is used to move files or directories, **Rename-Item** is used to rename a file or folder, and **Get-Content** can retrieve file contents. Finally, the **Test-Path** cmdlet can be used to check if a specific folder or file exists at the specified location.

PowerShell also offers several data and time operations, such as setting the system date using the **Set-Date** cmdlet. The following examples demonstrate the different operations on system date and time:

- To add another day to the current data and set the new date, the following cmdlet may be used:

set-date -Date (Get-Date).AddDays(1).

Similarly, it is also possible to get the system date through the use of the following cmdlet:

Get-Date

This gives the current date in a format containing the day, months, date, and time. The following image shows different ways of setting the date a day ahead or a day behind the current date.

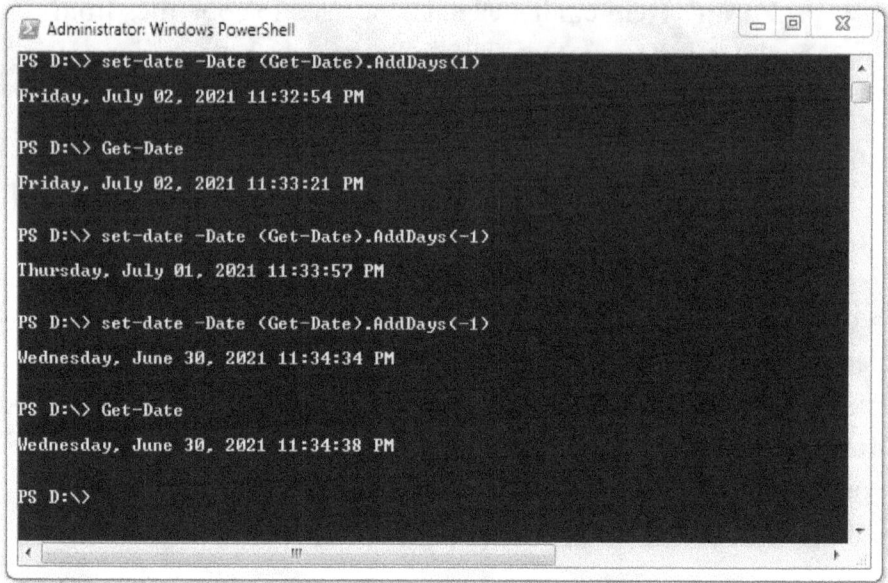

- In a similar manner, the system time can also be retrieved using the following cmdlet:

  Get-date -displayHint time displays the current time.

  In order to add sixty minutes to the current time, the following cmdlet syntax may be used:

  $timeAdded = New-TimeSpan -Minutes -60

  Set-Date -adjust $timeAdded

```
Administrator: Windows PowerShell
PS D:\> Get-date -displayHint time
11:35:56 PM

PS D:\> $timeAdded = New-TimeSpan -Minutes -60
PS D:\> Set-Date -adjust $timeAdded
Wednesday, June 30, 2021 10:36:44 PM

PS D:\>
```

Furthermore, PowerShell offers powerful I/O operations for different types of files. A simple sequence of cmdlets used to create a new file NewFile.txt, add some content, and print the contents of the file is included below:

New-Item D:\NewFile.txt

Set-Content D:\NewFile.txt 'This is a new file with some text'

Get-Content D:\MewFile.txt

PowerShell also allows several operations on common file types, such as CSV, XML, and HTML files. The following example shows brief information on the cmdlets used to work with XML files. In the example below, a new file called **MyTestFile.xml** is created, and a new tag is added with some content. Finally, the contents of the XML file are displayed. The sequence of steps are displayed below:

New-Item D:\MyFolder\MyTestFile.xml -ItemType File

Set-Content D:\MyFolder\MyTestFile.xml '<heading>This is a new Class</heading>'

Get-Content D:\MyFolder\MyTestFile.xml

Similar operations can be carried on CSV files as shown below. The sequence of steps demonstrated in the following cmdlets create a new file, add new content to the file, and display the content on the console:

New-Item D:\MyFolder\MyFile.csv -ItemType File

Set-Content D:\MyFolder\MyFile.csv 'Monday, Tuesday, Wednesday'

Get-Content D:\MyFolder\MyFile.csv

Another frequently used filetype is the HTML file, which can be created, edited, and displayed using a similar syntax:

New-Item D:\MyFolder\MyFile.html -ItemType File

Set-Content D:\MyFolder\MyFile.html '<html>This is a test file</html>'

Get-Content D:\MyFolder\MyFile.html

Two other important operations on files pertain to erasing the contents of the file and adding more content to the end of the file:

Clear-Content D:\MyTestFile.txt

Get-Content D:\MyTestFile.txt

Set-Content D:\MyTestFile.txt 'This is my life'

Add-Content D:\MyTestFile.txt 'story'

Get-Content D:\MyTestFile.txt

```
PS D:\> Clear-Content D:\MyFolder\MyFile.txt
PS D:\> Get-Content D:\MyFolder\MyFile.txt
PS D:\> Set-Content D:\MyFolder\MyFile.txt 'This is my life'
PS D:\> Add-Content D:\MyFolder\MyFile.txt 'story'
PS D:\> Get-Content D:\MyFolder\MyFile.txt
This is my life
story
PS D:\>
```

The cmdlets displayed above manipulate the contents of **MyTestFile.txt**. First, the contents of the file are cleared, and the file is displayed. This confirms that all the existing content in the file has been erased successfully. Thereafter, some new contents are added to the same file using the cmdlet **Set-Content**. Following this action, another word is added to the file using the **Add-Content** cmdlet. The last two commands append content to the existing file. Finally, all contents of the file are displayed in the output using the **Get-Content cmdlet**.

Chapter Summary

- Powerful scripting is supported by PowerShell through the use of variables, operators, arrays, looping, decision-making constructs, conditional statements, and regular expressions.

- Scripting is also useful in supporting operations on files and folders.

- Other common functions include setting the date and time and performing I/O operations to name a few.

Chapter Seven: Advanced Cmdlets in PowerShell

This chapter focuses on some of the advanced functions that can be performed using PowerShell cmdlets.

- To retrieve only the unique objects from a list that has already been sorted, the **Get-Unique** cmdlet can be used. In the following example, a variable is created to store color names. This list is printed then sorted. Finally, only the unique color names are printed:

$ColorList = "Red", "Blue", "Red", "Yellow", "Green"

$ColorList

$ColorList | Sort

$ColorList | Sort | Get-Unique

```
PS D:\> $ColorList = "Red", "Blue", "Red", "Yellow", "Green"
PS D:\> $ColorList
Red
Blue
Red
Yellow
Green
PS D:\> $ColorList | sort
Blue
Green
Red
Red
Yellow
PS D:\> $ColorList | sort | Get-Unique
Blue
Green
Red
Yellow
PS D:\>
```

- The **Start-Sleep** cmdlet instructs PowerShell to pause scripting for the time specified and resume afterward. The period to pause or sleep can be specified in either seconds, with a **-s** parameter, or in milliseconds with a **-m** parameter:

  Start-Sleep -s 5

  Start-Sleep -m 500

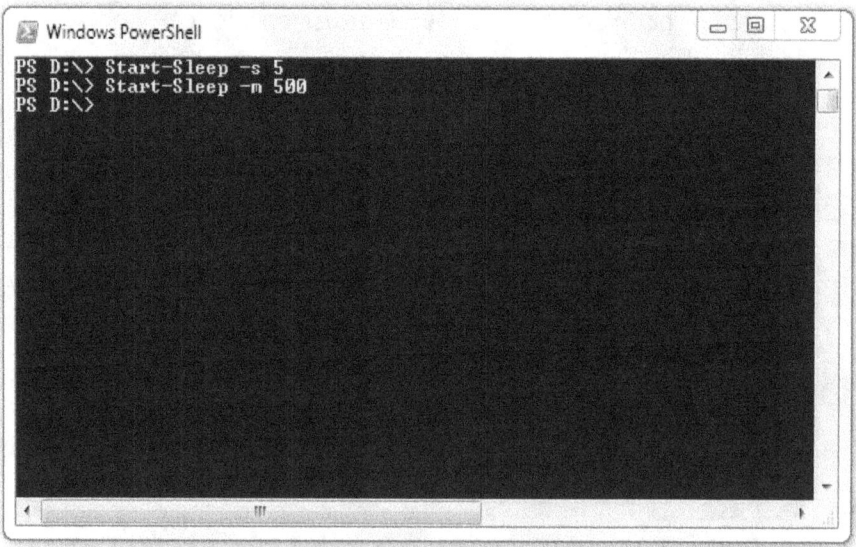

- It is also possible to measure how much time a script takes to execute in PowerShell. The **Measure-Command** cmdlet is used to accomplish this purpose. A simple command to retrieve the eventlog in PowerShell can be specified as follows:

  Measure-Command {Get-Eventlog "Windows PowerShell"}

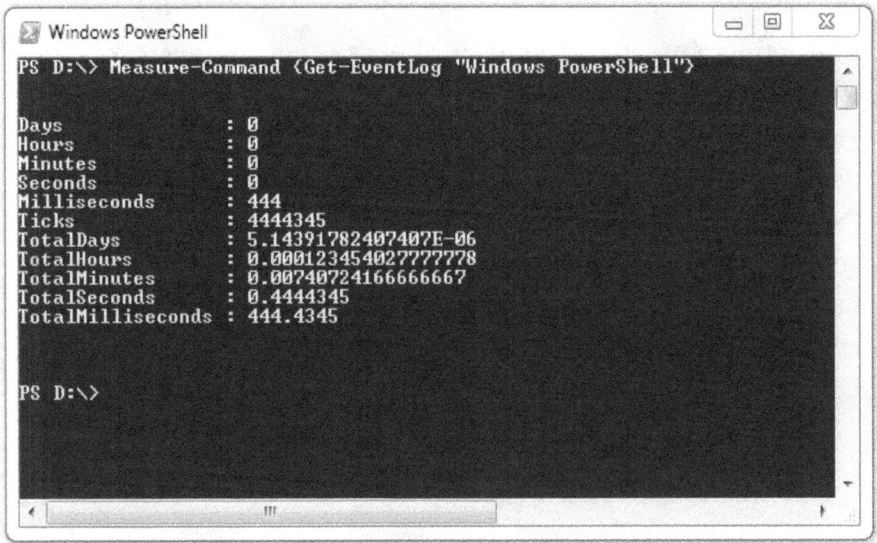

- Warning messages can be written in PowerShell using the **Write-Warning** cmdlet. An example is demonstrated below. The warning message is displayed with a unique color and background:

Write-Warning "New Warning"

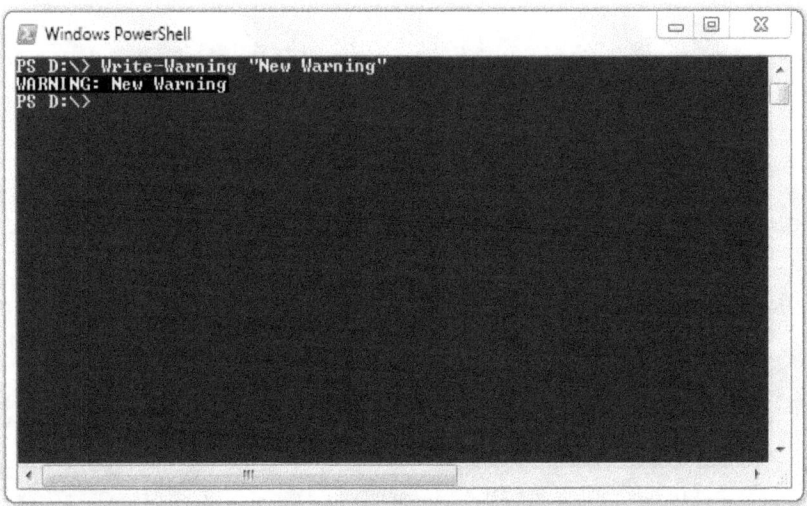

PowerShell offers several other advanced cmdlets for administering powerful systems. It offers system administrators with the capabilities that are characteristic of Bash scripting in Linux, which extends the functionality of Windows systems. The variables, decision-making constructs, looping structures, operators, cmdlets, and scripting support available in PowerShell make it a versatile programming environment. Administrators can take advantage of advanced built-in commands to execute scripts a single time or multiple times.

Chapter Summary

Some of the advanced cmdlets discussed in this chapter include:

- **Get-Unique** cmdlet to retrieve unique values from a list of values.

- **Start-Sleep** cmdlet, which causes PowerShell scripting to pause or sleep for the specified time period.

- **Measure-Command** cmdlet, which is used to measure the time taken to execute the script.

- **Write-Warning** cmdlet, which is useful in writing warning messages with a specific formatting.

Final Words

PowerShell is a convenient, command-based scripting interface designed for the Windows platform. It allows the use of simple scripts to take care of complex and critical administrative tasks. PowerShell offers a simple programming structure supporting variables, arrays, basic decision constructs, looping, and many more functions for administrators.

The simple yet powerful programming approach of PowerShell allows the execution of the desired services, security solutions, and operations on one or multiple servers. Scripts can be used to construct cmdlet pipelines and obtain the desired output and formatting using multiple cmdlets. It also offers several advanced cmdlets, which make it possible to complete complex administrative tasks in a fraction of the usual time and effort. It's simple yet powerful commands and functions make it extremely convenient for system administrators to take care of the most daunting system management tasks with the customization that they intend to achieve.

www.ingramcontent.com/pod-product-compliance
Lightning Source LLC
LaVergne TN
LVHW022003060526
838200LV00003B/69